Slut!

Letting Go of Shame
Surrounding Sex and Sexuality

Natasha Wilson, LMSW

Horizon Works

© 2024 by Natasha Wilson, LMSW

All rights reserved. This book or any portion thereof may not be reproduced or used in any manner whatsoever without the express written permission of the publisher except for the use of brief quotations in a book review.

Table of Contents

PREFACE 1
Nick 6
CHAPTER ONE: GETTING READY FOR THE WORK 8
Simone 10
CHAPTER TWO: PRACTICES IN MINDFULNESS 11
Hussein 19
CHAPTER THREE: CHANGING PROBLEMATIC THINKING 21
Elena 27
CHAPTER FOUR: ENEMIES OF HAPPINESS, JOY, AND GREAT SEX 29
Sam 37
CHAPTER FIVE: CONFLICTING FEELINGS, BELIEFS, AND IDENTITIES 39
Marie 47
CHAPTER SIX: KINK AND FETISH 49
Kenyel 52
CHAPTER SEVEN: QUEERNESS 55
Soleil 61
CHAPTER EIGHT: INTERSECTIONALITY OF RACE, SEXUAL ORIENTATION, AND GENDER 64
Jeremy 75
CHAPTER NINE: THE CHURCH 78
Amara 85
CHAPTER TEN: DISMANTLING RAPE CULTURE 87
Nicole 97
CHAPTER ELEVEN: ENDING LEGACIES OF SEXUAL SHAME 99
BIBLIOGRAPHY 102

Preface

The motivation to write this book innately developed through my personal and professional experiences. In my professional work as a psychotherapist, sex therapist, and life coach, many of the clients I work with have had difficult life experiences that have impacted their lives in many ways. The most commonly shared difficulties relate to sex, trauma, gender, and sexuality. These elements of a person's lived experience can affect various aspects of their lives. Many people have made positive transformations through the process of reflective examination to improve relationships with themselves, partners, and others. Shaming sexuality has harmful impacts on the lives of many people and can be enriched through open discussion and exploration. Fear only impedes growth and knowledge. The journey to heal and love the self can be a life-changing experience that transmutes needless self-harm to the joy of living in peace with your own existence, as you are.

Another is that my own life experiences have many intersectional elements that will be discussed in this text. In addition to my work as a licensed clinical therapist (LMSW), I embody several identities that have unique perspectives that lend understanding of the complexities of gender identity, sexual orientation and other social outliers. My experiences of being Black, genderqueer, kinky, lesbian, pagan, and privileged with being well-educated at elite institutions inform my perspectives and are the lived experience from which I understand the world. Admittedly, this is a bias that I am openly sharing.

I grew up in a middle class, mostly white neighborhood, and attended parochial schools through my childhood years. In this environment I was blessed with many advantages and challenges and have come to understand myself in different ways throughout various epochs of my life. I was told by my mother just before beginning kindergarten that there would be some people who simply wouldn't like me because I'm Black and to not take it to heart and to stand up for myself. I was five-years-old but it was necessary to have this information before I was exposed to the larger world for the first time. Having this support and knowledge was an armor that was tested and used countless times as I navigated school, puberty, microaggressions, homophobia, and racism while coming to make sense of who I am whilst simultaneously being bathed in the expectations and socialization of a world that is not always kind, welcoming, or validating.

Because of the way that I speak, the way I look, or my own idiosyncrasies, I found that I could experience rejection from people, regardless of whether they looked like me or not. This taught me to take people as individuals and to not assume someone is an ally or enemy based on their perceived identity. It was not uncommon to be rejected by some Black people because I talk like someone who grew up in suburban (mostly white) America. In the schools I attended, I was one of sometimes only a handful of brown kids. This was laden with the added awareness of the stereotypes that people have about Black people and how, although not bullied or targeted, I was also frequently made aware of being "other." This took some getting used to as a kid; like most kids, you just want to have friends and be accepted. If that were not enough, I always knew that I liked girls, but was unsure of how I felt about boys growing up. Everyone tells you that you will like boys and fall in love with your husband someday to live happily ever after. At least that's how the social narrative goes. This incessant heteronormative programming combined with fervid teenage hormones made figuring this out a bit complicated. Going back even further was the awareness that I never felt like a girl. The first time I was made aware of my gender was at age four when I was playing outside with some neighborhood boys and came back to the house and casually asked if I could pee on the trees like the other boys. My mother was apparently horrified at this question and forbade me from going back outside to play for the rest of the day. At age four, this seemed like a terrible injustice that I didn't understand (all day is a long time when you're four-years-old). She told me time and time again in my early years that I was a girl. But I insisted that I was a boy and that someday, she'll see! I knew who I was despite what everyone else told me I was to be. At age ten when I got my first period, I was absolutely devastated and angry (I still am) that I wasn't going to grow up to be a man. I remember watching my dad shave and being curious about the way he glided one of those old-style razors over his beard and I wanted to do the same too someday. To my horror, I was confined in this body that has never felt right. But in my prepubescence, I was not that different from the boys I played with. I loved wrestling, playing in the woods and getting dirty. I didn't have female friends until middle school because I didn't want to play with dolls or have tea parties like my sister. I liked physical play with boys because when you punched them, they laughed and didn't cry. It's funny the things you notice about yourself only in hindsight. It also made sense why I also loved pulling and snapping girl's bra straps so much. I delighted in hearing their squeals and admonishments only encouraged me more. This was foreshadowing of kinky things to come.

Fortunately, I was spared the struggle of wrestling with religious beliefs that made coming to understand myself more daunting. Being Black and born in the South meant that I was raised Baptist. This was regularly enforced. If you don't know about Black Baptist churches, it is a cultural phenomenon worthy of its own volume of exploration. However, for brevity, being socialized as female, it was expected that you wear the finest of dresses with tights, polished shoes, and expertly laid hair ornamented with age-appropriate bows and pigtails to church on Sunday. I *hated* it! Not only that, church on Sunday is an all-day endurance of sermons sometimes to be continued late into the evening, interrupted by an intermission for lunch at the church fellowship hall and then resumed with more sermons and choir singing. I could never buy into it. I heard all the stories, attended Wednesday Bible study and Sunday school before church even began, but there were too many inconsistencies that became increasingly apparent when I started to question and learn more about history and the world. I saw the hypocrisy, the gossip, pretense, and objectionable doctrines, until gradually, Christianity lost relevance in my life. I was drawn to spirituality and pagan traditions from around the world. At age fifteen, I began studying tarot, shamanism, and witchcraft. I felt alive and connected with the divine in a palpable way when I was communing with nature and sensing energies around me. From an early age, I felt connected to the natural world and was fortunate to have had the ability to roam freely unattended as a child through the woods, exploring and being a part of the land that too was alive. Nature is my sanctuary.

As I have matured into my adult years, the layered identities of sexual orientation, gender, race, sexuality, and spirituality have given me a richness that finds joy in helping others find the freedom that exists when you live authentically and with self-love and acceptance. Life is too short to live for everyone else but yourself. You deserve love and that begins with loving who you are as a person.

This book is written for anyone who feels discomfort, shame, or even mixed feelings related to sex and/or sexuality. Many people have been negatively influenced by messages of shame from society, religion, family, and other important influences in their lives. The intent is to find peace with whatever form of sexuality brings pleasure and joy to your life. How one achieves this is a personal journey. As you embark upon this journey toward self-acceptance, you may be challenged by the pervasiveness of self-limiting thoughts based in shame surrounding sex and sexuality. You may feel conflicted and afraid to let go of fundamental beliefs held throughout your life to the present despite their harm to your well-being. This is normal and expected. It is also possible to make peace with conflicting beliefs and find self-acceptance. You may have to let go of old ways of thinking in favor of new perspectives that allow for the integration of the multifaceted dimensions of your humanity. You may feel both loss and elation at the thought of this. It may also evoke discomfort and confusing thoughts/feelings. The experience of cognitive dissonance is not unexpected, as the process of change invites you to reflect upon thoughts, feelings, and beliefs that may be in direct conflict with each other yet also hold essential truths. Because this is to be expected, allow yourself to create space for reflection to examine your responses. This is the beginning of positive change that will pay dividends in the form of self-acceptance and inner peace.

Many thanks to the individuals who were so gracious as to allow me to share their stories of overcoming sexual repression! May their stories inspire you to be brave in allowing yourself to challenge beliefs that restrict you from complete acceptance of your sexuality without shame or guilt. This book weaves personal stories collected from individuals who have experienced some sort of challenge in overcoming barriers to sex positivity and acceptance. They serve to demonstrate that it is possible to overcome impediments to enjoying a happy and healthy sex life. It also offers information that hopefully will inspire those on the journey to self-acceptance of their sexuality. You are invited to challenge your beliefs and practice skills discussed in this text through reflective questions intended to inspire introspection. You may find it beneficial to engage in journaling practices to allow you to process your experiences further while engaging this text. A few pages are added to enable the reader to make notes related to their experiences and thoughts that may arise while working with this book.

My sincerest hope is that you will find your inner slut! Being a slut is to take ownership of your sexuality and to express it however you see fit, without shame or guilt. How you decide to do that is entirely up to you, whether in a married monogamous relationship or any other configuration of relationship(s). Embracing sex positivity is the means to deconstructing the prisons of shame and guilt. This process of change can be especially difficult for some who may have experienced trauma in addition to shaming belief systems. Take your time if you become triggered by any thought or feeling that may occur.

A note about how to approach this text: If you are new to therapeutic approaches such as how to intentionally calm and relax your body to soothe your mind, it is recommended that you explore the opening chapters on connecting with your body and breath. This simple engagement opens connection with the body to better understand parts of yourself that may have had to survive rather than thrive due to external influences beyond your control. This can be unsettling, at first, but is informative if you have held hurt in your body. By allowing yourself to tolerate this transitory discomfort, you are able to cleanse and free yourself of emotional injury and live with greater fullness of being. Many people who have engaged cognitive behavioral therapy with a mental health professional may be familiar with instructions on how to change problematic thoughts. If you feel competent in being able to recognize unhelpful thoughts and correct them reflexively, then you may wish to begin this text at Chapter 4: Enemies of happiness, joy, and great sex.

If you find that these cognitive reshaping and relaxation skills are not sufficient or that your experience of trauma is such that you feel unable to move forward on your own, I highly recommend seeking a qualified mental health professional/sex therapist to discuss your experiences and specific interventions that can be utilized to heal from sexual trauma

A brief disclaimer: You may be offended. I ask that you please allow this to happen and then observe what it is that offends and why? Where did these beliefs originate? Is this something you also believe is true, and why? This book is about exploration and discovery. I encourage you to brazenly challenge any belief system that has hindered your ability to enjoy sex and sexuality. This is not about dogma or debate about what is appropriate for one person or another. That is for you to decide. My intent is to nurture greater comfort and enjoyment of sex and sexuality in your life. This is no small task; it is a lifetime's journey for others. This book is written without judgment but with compassion for those who feel hindered from enjoying an essentially human experience. It is based upon the belief that sex is a human need and pleasure a human right. In essence, sex positivity!

Sex positivity can be described as a belief that sexuality is a healthy and natural part of human life and should not be feared, oppressed, or shamed. Sexuality is more than sexual orientation. It is the experience one has when experiencing sensual/sexual encounters, whether they be in real life or only in imagination or fantasy. This exploration of sexuality could include one's biological, emotional, and physical being, including social and spiritual connections for many people. Essentially, a person can be celibate and still have a sexual orientation. Do you remember having a crush or sexual desire for people of certain gender(s)/sex(es) before you ever had a sexual experience? Did you just know who you were generally attracted to without engaging in sexual activity? This general awareness could be described as a person's sexual orientation. Gender is separate from sex. Sex refers to biological traits associated with the human body in terms of being female or male. Gender, however, is much more nuanced. Gender entails a person's internal experience of themselves, reflecting traits associated with the spectrum ranging from being primarily masculine to feminine.

Given the spectrum of natural variances in human experiences, gender cannot be simplified into a binary assertion of humans being exclusively female or male. Sex and gender are often mistakenly conflated to mean the same things; however, they are distinct descriptions of a human experience. For some, this concept is foreign compared to what you may have been taught and socialized to understand. Maybe you are still exploring or are simply unsure? This book is intended to be a companion as you look within and explore the meaning, understanding, and awareness of yourself as a sexual being.

Human sexuality is a complicated and nuanced experience, varying from one individual to another, and it is also essential to acknowledge that some people are not primarily motivated by sexual interest of any gender or sex. Asexuality is also a valid sexual orientation. We will explore various aspects of sex, sexual orientation, and gender.

You may discover that what was presented as simplistic categories of a person's identity and experiences are much more multifaceted. The promotion of sex positivity is not to say that people are free to do whatever they like without consequences, simply that every individual has the right to choose how they would like to engage sexuality without judgment. To be explicitly clear, all sexual experiences promoted in this text are in reference to sexual activity between consenting adults. Consent allows each person to choose what consequences, behaviors, or expressions they feel are best for them. Consent is also sexy. It allows participants to clearly state their desires and the boundaries that should be respected. This is a foundational belief and understanding. For some, this could be negotiating sexual boundaries within a queer, kinky, and polyamorous partnership. For others, this could be finding pleasure that is satisfying to an individual in a monogamously married heterosexual relationship or any other variety of relationships, including that with the self.

This book is truly intended to assist anyone who may benefit from dismantling barriers to happy and healthy sexual lives. This is inclusive of people of all sexual orientations, genders, ethnic, or religious backgrounds.

Nick

AGE: 23, WHITE, CISGENDERED, QUEER, GAMER NERD, WOMAN, RAISED IN A CONSERVATIVE CHRISTIAN HOUSEHOLD

I went from being a young Christian girl to a queer anarchist. My parents were true believers who took the Bible as God's word and were highly involved in the Evangelical church. Growing up I knew what my church and parents believed but also knew that I was queer. This made me feel isolated from my peers at church and I never really got along with them. I suppose they always knew I was different. Life started to change in middle school when I met people from other communities and some of them were not from religious homes. By getting to know people with different beliefs, I began to question the beliefs that I had been taught from a young age. I just didn't think that my friends deserved to go to hell. This started unraveling my belief in the fundamentals of the faith I was raised believing. I just couldn't believe that the same people who were kind and open to accepting me as I am, were damned for all eternity. My dissolving faith caused conflicts with my family who insisted that I still attend church each week. Having no choice at the moment, I complied but I continued to explore my own identity separate from the limited vision my parents had for me. Finally, my parents started to put the pieces together and asked me if I was gay? I said yes, and they cried. My sister was amazing and accepted me from the beginning. Unfortunately, my parents did not. It still hurts that I can't just be myself and have them love me all the same.

My girlfriend was barred from coming to the house, but I was not forbidden from meeting with her. However, I was not able to stay over at someone else's place, I had to be home. The shame and pressure my parents placed on me made life difficult. Yet, strict parents just raise good liars. I was able to get around their demands by saying I was participating in various activities and groups but was meeting my girlfriend nearly every weekend. Even now, years after coming out to my family, we still don't talk about it. I would love to be able to be my full authentic self with my parents but that is just not possible. They would not understand, nor do they want to. That much has been made clear. After years of being made to feel that I am deviant and inherently wrong, I realized that I needed to address the internalized shame that was placed on me by my upbringing. It was a process of self-examination and questioning the origins of beliefs that no longer aligned with the world as I know it. I feel free to not be constrained by the dogma imposed on me by my family. I am able to see more beauty in the world without judgmental biases. More importantly, I can accept myself and to love who I love regardless of other people's beliefs. If I were able to talk to my thirteen-year-old self, I would tell her that I turned out to be cool. I would advise her to surround herself with people who accept you and the importance of self-expression.

CHAPTER ONE
Getting ready for the work

Building coping skills for relaxation, mindfulness, and grounding

During the process of engaging this book, you may feel discomfort and uncertainty regarding how you feel. This is normal and even expected if you have carried shame regarding sexuality for some time. To begin this journey, a few relaxation and self-soothing exercises have been included to address uncomfortable feelings that may arise through engaging your thoughts and experiences. Remember, conflicting thoughts/feelings are expected to occur. You may feel discomfort/trepidation. It can feel unsettling, but this will shift and change with time and engagement of reflections throughout this text. Such thoughts regarding sex/sexuality have been so pervasive in your life that you may not have questioned them until recently. This is something that happens in various stages of life for many people. You may be a young person who is discovering yourself as a sexual being, or you may be later in life and are finally coming to a place where you feel free to be your true self. All of these experiences are valid and acceptable. So be patient with yourself and the process of changing how you think and feel. To receive the best results from these exercises, daily practice is best. This can be done by dedicating between 5-15 minutes per day to reflect upon questions that arise, as well as practicing relaxation/grounding skills to assist with challenging moments in this very personal journey.

Sexuality encompasses more than assigning classification to a person's sexual desires and inclinations. It shapes one's experience of the world in intimate ways that sometimes are only known to the self. These self-reflections and comparisons often color our understanding of ourselves and others. Living in a society that is not sex-positive tends to instill beliefs that may be counterproductive to fully accepting oneself as you are, a fully sexual human being. At times, this journey of discovery can be somewhat unsettling. However, mindfulness and centeredness can assist you with managing these emotional experiences.

Mindfulness is the awareness of one's thoughts, feelings, and the environment surrounding a person in the present moment. Most importantly, it brings a person to the present moment without judgment. By paying attention to the present moment, you can gain better insight and understanding of your experiences. How is this done? It involves directing your attention to your experiences, both internal and external, to yourself, paying attention to the mundane. In our busy lives, it is typical to feel divided between various work, family, school, career, or child-rearing obligations. The practice of mindfulness intentionally slows the pace of your awareness to allow quiet reflection and noticing of your own thoughts, feelings, and sensory experiences. Instead of moments where you may be mindlessly doing a task while thinking about what comes next, you stay in the present moment to experience aspects of being that go unnoticed otherwise. Have you ever tasted food with your eyes closed? What could you taste that might have ordinarily gone unnoticed if you were to do so? This engagement of awareness in the present moment is mindfulness. Incorporating this practice into your daily life allows you to experience and engage yourself and the world around you with greater intentionality. I have included examples of mindfulness practices that can assist you with beginning this practice of self-discovery.

Simone

AGE: 33, BLACK, HETEROSEXUAL, WORLD TRAVELER, CISGENDERED, WOMAN

I didn't grow up in a particularly religious household. My parents didn't regularly go to church, but I was taught that I belonged to the Christian faith. Mainly, this was the cultural norm where I grew up, so it was easy to fit in with peers in my community. Growing up in my hometown in Ohio, I just didn't feel it was a place that I could fit into or could get much out of. I was popular and got along with most people, but I just wasn't satisfied with the limited opportunities in my town and wanted to experience more. When I finished school, I worked for a bit and then moved to Chicago. Here, I was able to connect with people from various ethnic and religious backgrounds, and I found a place where I can just be and not feel judged by people. After having time away from where I grew up, I was able to reflect upon the beliefs of the Christian faith, and it's just not something that I subscribe to anymore. I just believe in treating people with kindness and being a good person.

I'm also not a very political person. I don't really get into labels about sexuality or beliefs. Generally, I consider myself to be a straight woman. However, I have had sexual experiences with other women. I'm not interested in having a relationship with a woman and wouldn't think of myself as being queer. I am primarily attracted to men and would prefer a relationship with a man. Finding language to describe my experiences can be tricky and can be somewhat overwhelming for me. I didn't know the word heteroflexible until our discussion, but I suppose it would be accurate. It's so great that there are so many ways to conceptualize oneself! There are so many new labels and words to describe sexuality now that weren't available until more recently. The world I grew up in didn't really have these words or open discussions about sexuality. Being straight is the norm, and there wasn't much room for questioning. Because I've always thought of myself as being straight, defining myself sexually wasn't something that I felt invested in. I just didn't have the context and language to think outside of social expectations at the time. It's nice to be able to do that and have a better understanding of human experiences. I'm happy with my life now and enjoy being immersed in different cultures and people. I couldn't imagine myself going back to living in the place where I grew up.

CHAPTER TWO
Practices in mindfulness

Exercise: Being present for your breath

Breathing is something that many take for granted, but it is one of the most centering tools at your disposal, given that it is available to you at any time and in any place free of charge. The availability to utilize your breath to soothe feelings of discomfort will benefit you along this journey and beyond. You may find this to be helpful when managing difficult feelings. Emotions sometimes occur without having a clear understanding of their origin or cause. Developing this skill offers a route to self-soothing feelings that may rise unexpectedly or seemingly without provocation. You may feel triggered or emotionally unsettled by having feelings that are unexpectedly strong in response to something you may encounter in this practice or in life in general. Your breath allows you to relax your mind and your body and center your awareness. From this place of centered calm, you can best examine what elicits this experience? This reflection opens the possibility of effectively gaining insight into what is at the core of this emotional response. Here is where you can examine concepts/ beliefs that complicate the ability to experience unconditional love and self-acceptance for the self. Here is where healing is possible.

Research published in the National Library of Medicine explored the effects of meditative breath on the body. Not surprisingly, it confirmed knowledge that has been known to various cultures around the world for thousands of years: that engaging the breath in slow, intentional practice has positive physiological and psychological effects (NIH.gov, 2017). In overly simplistic terms, our nervous system (brain, spinal cord, and peripheral nerves) engages the primary functions of activation and relaxation, sympathetic and parasympathetic responses. The experience of stress tends to activate the sympathetic nervous system, which prepares the body to respond to potential threats. Such activation would include widening of pupils, increased heart rate and blood pressure, and in-creased lung capacity. In contrast, the parasympathetic system acts to relax the body and produces a calming effect on the mind. This would include lower blood pressure and heart rate, digestion, and decreased respiration. These systems work to maintain balance in our bodies. Utilizing the breath is a method to intentionally activate parasympathetic responses, promoting relaxation of the body, and calming the mind. In our modern lives, most of us do not regularly encounter life-threatening situations. However, we are frequently bombarded with stressful situations. This tends to have adverse effects on one's sense of well-being. It is vital to both your well-being and work throughout this book to take a moment to breathe and allow yourself to connect with your inner being, to reflect upon your experiences, and how to can actively work to release yourself from shame surrounding sex and sexuality. Many people share the feeling that they do not have the time for regular self-care in their busy lives. However, this is not true. It is possible to find one minute to focus on your breath and connect with yourself in a relaxed state. This is less time than it takes to microwave a frozen meal for lunch. It would be beneficial to allow yourself to take several one-minute breaks throughout the day to reset your mental clarity and take a momentary respite from the stresses of daily life.

For the purpose of learning a new practice, take a moment to find a comfortable place to be, whether you are sitting or standing. If you become lightheaded or dizzy, simply find a place to sit and allow your breath to return to normal. If you are not used to taking deep breaths, it is not uncommon to have this experience. For most people, this is simply the effect of your brain receiving more oxygen than you may be used to. Of course, if this causes any significant physical distress, discontinue the practice, and discuss this with your doctor.

Begin by drawing a breath deep into your chest, filling it fully, and noticing your chest rise. As you draw in this breath, notice the feeling of filling your body with air and allowing its natural rhythm to gently allow you to relax, and let go of tension. When you notice that you have reached a maximum inhalation through your nose, take a moment to be aware of the moment just before your body exhales, ideally a bit slower than you inhaled. As you exhale, allow the muscles of your body to relax, lowering tight shoulders or relaxing a jaw that may hold tension. Notice when you feel the need to draw in another breath, repeat internally (or externally if needed): "Inhale" …... "Exhale" ….. and repeat. This can also be done in a series of four cycles of breathing in and out. This is commonly referred to as "square breathing." In this example, you may visualize your breath forming a square as you inhale and exhale.

A beautiful thing about using the breath as a meditation is that it can be engaged anywhere, at any time, whether alone or with others. There's nothing outwardly strange about someone breathing, and it costs nothing.

Exercise: Using your five senses and breathing mindfully

Take a moment to observe your five senses: taste, smell, touch, hearing, and sight. In this moment, can you identify at least one of each of these sensations? Now, come back to your breath and observe as your chest rises and fills with air. Bring your awareness to your breath as it transitions from inhalation to exhalation. Take a moment to allow this breath and moment of stillness to sit within your chest before slowly letting your breath escape and release any tension as you exhale. As you engage in this practice of mindfulness, allow each moment to pass without lingering on any one experience to the next. Allow your awareness to be centered on the current moment. This takes some practice. Most people will experience some amount of distraction when beginning this practice. No worry. When you notice that your awareness has wandered from the present moment, just come back to the attention of your breath and breathe. When distraction occurs, take note of the distraction and move on. After you have engaged in this awareness, what did you notice? Was there a theme or particular distraction that was difficult to ignore? Just take notice without judgment. Like any other skill, practice allows for better performance. When you notice yourself drifting from the present awareness, give yourself praise for noticing and continue engaging in the present moment!

Exercise: Mindfulness walk

In this exercise, you are encouraged to allow yourself to take a walk somewhere you feel comfortable. As you are walking along, challenge yourself to stay in the present. From each moment to the next, take note of what you are observing around you, naming what you observe with a simple word, and then move to the next moment, taking notice again of what you observe, naming each observation as they occur. If your mind wanders into a tangent, gently notice this and return to breathing and being aware of the next moment. Doing this will allow you to better observe your thoughts and beliefs with greater awareness and less judgment. This could look like walking down a familiar street in your neighborhood, meditatively breathing, and noticing a car speeding through a residential street. It would be tempting to let your mind wander to thoughts such as how that driver should slow down or how you might like their car. However, in this practice, you are tasked with simply saying to yourself, "car" and moving on to the next moment of your walking meditation experience.

Remember, you did not choose the society you were born into or the parents who raised you. Therefore, you must let go of feeling 100 percent responsible for the nonsense you came to believe due to your experiences. Now is the opportunity to free yourself of unnecessary baggage that hinders you from being your sensual and sexy self! Utilizing this practice will allow you to be more cognizant of thoughts that perpetuate shame and needless self-reproach.

Exercise: Mindful awareness

Practice engaging mindfulness throughout your day, particularly when you are doing ordinary tasks that do not require your full attention. An example might be challenging yourself to stay present in the shower. Resist thinking about your lists of the day or thoughts about what you will do next. Stay present. Can you notice the smell of the soap? The sound of the water? The feel of the water as it splashes about your body? Can you feel the warmth or steam? When you are eating food or doing the dishes, try to describe each aspect of the activity to yourself. Could you notice the warmth of the suds as you do the dishes? Stay present. It's easy to allow the mind to wander. It is the practice of noticing, being present and resisting judgment that will allow you to fully engage the practice of letting go of shame surrounding sex and sexuality. By engaging this practice, you will begin to notice the beliefs and thoughts that are so automatic that you may not have even stopped to question the origins of these edicts and whether or not you truly believe them. Do they hinder your ability to fully accept yourself? If so, they may need further examination. This comes from the belief that everyone has the right to accept and enjoy themselves as sexual beings. Sex positivity is one of the goals of this text. The goal of this journey is to embrace yourself as you are and to allow yourself pleasure in whatever form suits you best.

The chakras: an energetic practice

If you are inclined to experience the world with an empathic awareness of others and yourself, you have likely been aware of someone's energy or vibe you feel when they are in your presence. Having this same awareness of your body and your energy can be helpful in understanding the boundaries of where you end and another person begins. This awareness can be used to gain insight into where energy can be open or stuck within your energetic being. For example, a person who has felt unable to freely speak regarding their thoughts/experiences may feel blocked in their throat chakra. A person who has survived trauma in their body, particularly of a sexual nature, may similarly experience difficulties surrounding their sacral chakra. This does not mean that all who have had such experiences will have such blockages, only that it is not uncommon. Being aware of the flow of energy between these energy centers allows a person to direct healing attention toward various areas of the body as needed. It is widely understood that our experiences of trauma or injury have a way of lingering beyond the healing of the physical body; sometimes, these injuries are felt energetically within the body. Allowing yourself to connect your awareness to your body and its physical and energetic aspects can offer healing and a renewed connection to your body as a sexual being. If you are no longer in a harmful or abusive situation, it may take a moment to allow your body to relax and feel safe. Continued practice offers the opportunity to reclaim your body, inhabiting it without fear.

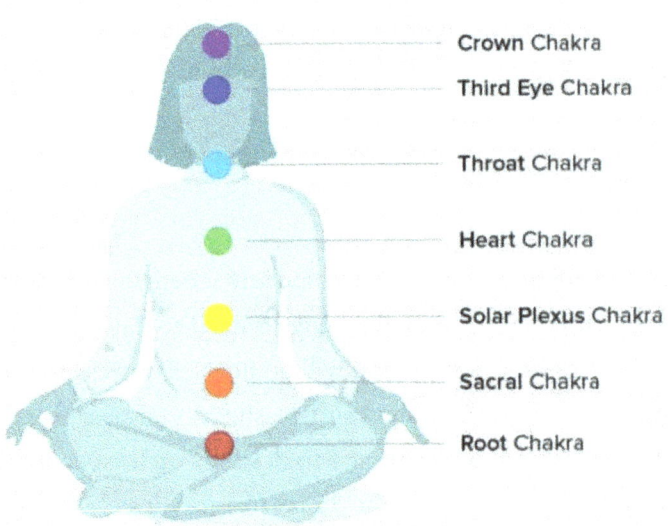

There is value in being able to connect with yourself mentally/emotionally, physically, and energetically. Connecting with yourself in this manner is a way to honor your ability to sit with awareness within your body and address energy imbalances should they arise. This is important because a part of being comfortable with sexuality is also having comfort with your own body. If you would like to approach chakra work in its most elemental form, connecting with the associated energy centers in your body teaches harmony within the self. Repression and shame act to create disharmony within the self. This is a method of connecting with your body and its energetic needs. It would not be possible to fully explain the chakras within this text. However, a basic description is that there are seven commonly acknowledged primary centers of energy within the body (although some traditions recognize more) that are associated with specific colors and elemental symbols. These energy centers correspond to different aspects of our being. When these energy centers are in alignment, we are able to feel the most balanced. Here is a description of these energy centers (Healthline 2022). The names associated with these chakras come from the Sanskrit language.

Root Chakra

The root chakra, or Muladhara, is located at the base of your spine. It provides you with a base or foundation for life, and it helps you feel grounded and able to withstand challenges. Your root chakra is responsible for your sense of security and stability.

Sacral Chakra

The sacral chakra, or Svadhisthana, is located just below your belly button. This chakra is responsible for your sexual and creative energy. It's also linked to how you relate to your emotions as well as the emotions of others.

Solar Plexus Chakra

The solar plexus chakra, or Manipura, is located in your stomach area. It's responsible for feelings of confidence and self-esteem, helping you feel in control of your life.

Heart Chakra

The heart chakra, or Anahata, is located near your heart, in the center of your chest. Unsurprisingly, the heart chakra is all about our ability to love and show compassion.

Throat Chakra

The throat chakra, or Vishuddha, is located in your throat. This chakra has to do with our ability to communicate verbally.

Third Eye Chakra

The third eye chakra, or Ajna, is located between your eyes. You can thank this chakra for a strong gut instinct. That's because the third eye is responsible for intuition. It's also linked to imagination.

Crown Chakra

The crown chakra, or Sahasrara, is located at the top of your head. Your Sahasrara represents your spiritual connection to yourself, others, and the universe. It also plays a role in your life's purpose.

Meditation practice: tree meditation for grounding

This meditation can be done in a quiet place or in nature. Take a seat on the ground or floor. Begin by connecting with your breath by observing the slow and natural rhythm of inhalation and exhalation. Take in a few more breaths, and then close your eyes. You will maintain this slow and peaceful breathing throughout the exercise. Now, imagine that you are connected to the earth by the extension of the tail of your spinal column into the ground. Like a tree, your roots (spinal tail) burrow into the earth and begin to spread outward as it reaches downward. When you feel that you can no longer reach outward or downward, sit and feel the connection with the earth beneath you. Imagine that you are a tree and can absorb all of the energy of the earth, drawing its nourishment within. Drink from this source of support and warmth. As you draw from the energy of this connection, pull that energy up through your spinal roots and allow it to fill your chakras as it rises through all the chakras from the root to the solar plexus, to the heart, throat, third eye, and finally extending upward through your crown chakra. When you imagine this energetic light extending throughout your entire body, allow this light and warmth to expand through the top of your head toward the skies above. Feel the connection as you are fully rooted in the earth and connected to the sky above. This is a great moment for feeling strength and connection to all that surrounds you. In this moment of deep connection, you may feel gratitude and the awareness of how supported you are, even when you feel alone. There remains the earth beneath your feet, the breath within your chest, and connection to the world surrounding you.

It would not be possible to fully explain the chakras within this text. However, a basic description is that there are seven primary energy centers within the body, although some traditions recognize more. These energy centers relate to different aspects of our being. When these energy centers are in alignment, we are able to feel the most balanced.

Recommendation:

Journaling your thoughts and observations from the mindfulness walk exercise may be helpful not only to process your present experience but also to offer insight into yourself, your beliefs, and your thoughts. Continuing this practice as you reflect upon your thoughts about yourself, and others provides the opportunity to develop greater self-acceptance and enjoyment of your sexuality. If this is new or not immediately easy to do, relax, breathe, and know that it will become more natural as you become more practiced with the experience of being present to the inner and outer world around you.

Furthermore, there are immediate, intermediate, and long-term benefits of journaling. An immediate benefit of journaling is to be able to vent and allow emotions to be processed. Here is where you can unleash all of the thoughts that are circling your mind. Give them a place to reside so your mind can rest better. An intermediate benefit is that after a while, you may notice themes or patterns in your writing. Perhaps this could reveal more progress than you initially realized. It could also indicate where you may be stuck and could benefit from discussing your thoughts with a trusted friend or professional. In the long term, having a record of your thoughts and feelings over time will allow you to witness how you have changed with time. Additionally, you will be able to reflect on how interactions with yourself and others change as you are better able to adopt a more positive and loving self-concept.

Reflection Questions:

Have you previously worked with your breath to engage relaxation? Which relaxation practices have been most beneficial to you in the past? How were they helpful to you?

_____
_____
_____
_____
_____

How often are you incorporating your practices throughout your week? Are there any changes you would like to make?

_____
_____
_____
_____
_____

If you have not dedicated a particular time for relaxation practices, when might you begin being able to do so? Which practices would be the easiest to begin? Which one would you like to do but do not have the ability to engage at the present?

_____
_____
_____
_____
_____

What are the obstacles that make such practices difficult? Can you identify any potential solutions to remove such obstacles? What could change? How could things be different?

_____
_____
_____
_____
_____

Are there any concessions or compromises that might make this more accessible for you?

_____
_____
_____
_____
_____

Is it difficult to prioritize yourself? If so, could you consider how a healthier you may be better able to benefit those most important in your life? What would you wish for someone you truly loved?

_____
_____
_____
_____
_____

Hussein

AGE: 31, IRANIAN REFUGEE, MUSLIM, GAY, MALE, SOCIAL SERVICE WORKER, UNSURE OF GENDER

Growing up in Iran, being gay was not something that anyone ever acknowledged or discussed. My parents were traditional and conservative Muslims. I was expected to grow up, get married, and have children. This is what was expected of me, especially as the only son. When I was younger, I didn't understand why or how I was different; I just knew I was. I would rather spend time with my mother in the house cooking than doing the things boys my age were doing. When I got a bit older, it was harder to deny who I was, and I also knew that if anyone were to find out, it would cause shame upon my family and that I could be violently rejected by my parents. I was, however, close with my sister.

I was able to confide in my sister, who loved me but was still not accepting of my homosexuality. She was preparing to get married and was fearful that the groom's family would find out and back out of the wedding. She begged me not to tell anyone. I understood, and I wanted her to get married and be happy. I think my mother knew but never said anything. She encouraged me to do well in school and was kind and loving. My father was much more stern and was not one to communicate or easily empathize with anything contrary to what he believed was right. One day, he confronted me about being gay, and I immediately denied it, but he didn't believe me. He beat me and kicked me out of the house that day. I left and eventually found people who helped me while I figured out what to do next. Since I had nothing and no family connections, I left and was granted asylum in the United States. Coming here took a long time to become adjusted, but I love that I can be openly gay and not be condemned by everyone around me. It's also why I now work for a nonprofit that helps other refugees from the Middle East.

Adjusting to life here involved not only learning English, settling into an apartment, and navigating finding work; it was a complete culture shock. I was able to go to school and now have a partner. One thing I haven't been able to get used to is how sexualized gay pride events can be. I just don't think that should be something that should be out in the streets. Perhaps it's from my upbringing, but I'm just not comfortable with it. My partner is also Muslim; however, we are not religious. It's more of a cultural identity than practice for me now.

When asked about gender, this is not something I am not really able to answer at this point in my life. There are aspects of myself that are softer and perhaps somewhat feminine, but I have never identified as being a woman. The concept of gender is hard for me to fully comprehend, so I just identify as being a man.

My sister did get married, but I lost contact with her some years ago. I hope she is happy, and I don't hold any hard feelings against her or anyone in my family. I enjoy living in peace.

CHAPTER THREE
Changing problematic thoughts

Introduction to the Thought Record

Okay, now that you've had some practice observing your thoughts/feelings, what did you notice? Were there any persistent thoughts/experiences that were notable for you? And even more importantly, what to do with them?? Now that errant/negative thoughts/feelings have been identified, let's work with them to examine their truth and impact on your well-being. For example, I may have been taught to wait until marriage to have sex, and now that I'm married, it's hard to let go and just enjoy myself. What notions can be extinguished? What could you replace them with instead?

Sometimes, it is necessary to dig a little deeper beyond the obvious answers. Ask yourself not only what thoughts are identified but also what do they mean/say about you? What assumptions are built upon these core beliefs? Core beliefs are foundational beliefs that lie beneath our assumptions and expectations. An example of a core belief may be that "I am not worthy." Based upon this belief, I may assume that I do not deserve the same as others. As a result of this belief, I come to experience that others take advantage of me, and I feel resentful. By examining this chain of connected beliefs, I can intervene and challenge any part of them for errors in thought or judgment. Can you spot the errors in this example? How might you rephrase them instead? These are called reframed thoughts. A reframed thought is not simply "think positive" things. Instead, it is a gradual adjustment of faulty beliefs that can be altered to be more helpful or less self-critical. In the beginning, such reframing may not sound overwhelmingly positive. That is okay and perfectly acceptable. What is most important is that you are able to correct these thoughts in a more positive manner, even if the immediate conceptualization is not all sunshine and rainbows! What is most important is that this is an improvement of the previously held belief toward something you can connect with yet still feels true. An example of these alterations could be, "Although I don't see myself as being beautiful, occasionally other people compliment me." This thought doesn't state that "I'm beautiful just the way I am!" but opens the possibility for there being some truth to the concept that others may not see me as being as unattractive as I may internally feel. See the difference? The Thought Record tool is helpful in distilling beliefs into foundational thoughts so that they may be challenged and changed accordingly.

Although it may be tempting to just try to think these out in your mind, I strongly recommend writing them out, at least initially. By writing your thoughts/beliefs in black and white on paper, you see these words written in your own handwriting and can more objectively see the errors in thoughts or assumptions. This offers an opportunity to challenge and change these thoughts into ones that are more loving and self-accepting. This process can be challenging at first, but with continued practice and patience, you will come to a place where you no longer need to write out these thoughts because you will find yourself correcting them in real-time. You will more readily notice negatively patterned thinking and reflexively change the tone or content of those thoughts. This can be quite life changing. And that is the point. By examining the origins and validity of negative self-reflections, you enable yourself to be free, to accept yourself, and even come to enjoy who you are as a person. This therapeutic intervention comes from the practice of cognitive behavioral therapy (CBT). CBT is an evidence-based practice, meaning that it has been utilized by numerous mental health practitioners with a multitude of clients and has consistently been shown to be effective. This approach is most widely utilized by mental health clinicians for this reason. So, let's get into it!

How to use a Thought Record

The first column of the thought record asks you to identify the situation of the event. What is the context of when you had a particular unhelpful/negative thought? What was the who, what, where, and why of the situation at hand? Placing these thoughts and experiences in context gives a proper understanding of how they can be interpreted.

The second column asks you to identify your feelings/emotions and to rate each feeling on a scale of intensity from 0 to 100. 100 represents the most intensely you could experience this feeling. Sometimes, people initially confuse thoughts with emotions. Feelings should be able to be captured in a single word most of the time, and thoughts tend to be expressed with sentences. This is a helpful guideline if you are unsure of how to categorize thoughts and feelings.

The third column asks you to identify your negative or unhelpful thoughts. Sometimes, our thoughts aren't solely in words. You may have a more visual imagination and have a thought that is expressed as an image. In this case, describe the image in this section of the thought record.

The fourth column asks you to find evidence that supports this thought being true. What are the reasons that make this thought to be convincing or true? Once you have exhausted all of the reasons that you believe a thought to be true, take a breath. It may be necessary to take a break or walk away from this exercise just to clear your head.

When you move to the fifth column, challenge yourself to find any evidence that does not support your original thought. This means that even if it is only partially untrue, it must be considered. Most likely, you will find errors in your unhelpful thought. This means that the old thought must be amended in order for the contradictory evidence to be more balanced or accurate. Remember, this section of the thought record doesn't require that the reframed thought be overwhelmingly positive or cheerful. It is intended to be more balanced and hopefully more self-accepting.

The sixth column is where you reframe your unhelpful thoughts to become more balanced and compassionate toward yourself. Here is where you may experience the cognitive dissonance of both recognizing how there are inconsistencies or errors in your beliefs that are made clearer through this exercise yet may still feel true. This is a state where you both feel that something false is true despite being aware of the evidence to the contrary. Cognitive dissonance is an expected experience of someone changing how they see themselves and the world that shaped their understanding. This can be scary and may feel wrong. But remember, despite what you may have been told, you are a human being deserving of love from yourself and others. Most importantly, even if no one in your community or social group views you as deserving of love, then you must be the person to affirm your inherent worth and value. This is critical for many who may feel isolated and alone. happen to live in a place that is not welcoming of sex positivity, it is easy to feel despair that there is no place for you. However, know that you are not alone and that there is a larger world where you may find a like-minded community. Assuming that you are not harming others in any manner, it is safe to say that you are not the worst human to have ever lived. If you can elevate your self-concept even higher than that, great! As you engage in this journey of self-acceptance and love, you will begin to find more compassion and less negative judgment of the self. This compassion grows within and affects how you engage the world around you. There gradually becomes less room in your thoughts and feelings for shame and self-degradation. You may also find that this transformation has the potential to extend toward many of the mistruths that have been masquerading as truth in your life and beliefs. Embrace this. Life is best when you are evolving to be the best version of yourself. If making such changes seems uncomfortable in any way, use this as motivation toward being a better person to the people you love to find the ability to love and accept yourself for who you are as a person. By giving yourself greater self-acceptance and unconditional love, you are best able to do the same for others as well.

Lastly, in the seventh column, you are asked to identify and rate the intensity of your feelings now that you have considered this alternative thought once again. Hopefully, by the end of this process, you will be able to formulate thoughts that are more kind and accepting of the self. However, this practice must be repeated frequently to be most effective. This could include writing a reframed/ balanced thought on paper and placing it somewhere you are likely to encounter it during your daily life.

Situation / Trigger	Feelings Emotions – (Rate 0 – 100%) Body sensations	Unhelpful Thoughts / Images	Facts that support the unhelpful thought	Facts that provide evidence against the unhelpful thought	Alternative, more realistic and balanced perspective	Outcome Re-rate emotion
What happened? Where? When? Who with? How?	What emotion did I feel at that time? What else? How intense was it? What did I notice in my body? Where did I feel it?	What went through my mind? What disturbed me? What did those thoughts/images/memories mean to me, or say about me or the situation? What am I responding to? What 'button' is this pressing for me? What would be the worst thing about that, or that could happen?	What are the facts? What facts do I have that the unhelpful thought/s are totally true?	What facts do I have that the unhelpful thought/s are NOT totally true? Is it possible that this is opinion, rather than fact? What have others said about this?	STOP!! Take a breath.... What would someone else say about this situation? What's the bigger picture? Is there another way of seeing it? What advice would I give someone else? Is my reaction in proportion to the actual event? Is this really as important as it seems?	What am I feeling now? (0-100%) What could I do differently? What would be more effective? Do what works!. Act wisely. What will be most helpful for me or the situation? What will the consequences be?

www.getselfhelp.co.uk   Carol Vivyan 2010, adapted from Padesky 1995. Permission to use for therapy purposes   www.get.gg

You are welcome to print copies of this chart and utilize it regularly as you are learning to deconstruct unhelpful thoughts related to the self, the world at large and particularly your place within it. You may also find value in going to the source of this document that has been shared by Carol Vivyan at: www.getselfhelp.co.uk. Remember, this is a gradual process that requires regular practice to be most effective!

Meditative visualization exercise:

Find a comfortable place to allow yourself the ease of closing your eyes and to be uninterrupted for less than 5 minutes. As you settle into a comfortable place, take a slow, deep breath into your nose, completely filling your chest. Upon exhalation, try to feel your body relax and release all tension out through your breath. As you are releasing this cleansing breath from your body, allow any tight muscles to relax as well. Try lowering your shoulders and letting your back or jaw let go of any tension. Feel free to repeat this moment of relaxation, breathing for longer if needed. When you are able, place your hands over your heart or heart chakra and think of someone you love dearly. As you visualize this person(s), smile sweetly to yourself as you imagine your own heart swelling with the love and adoration you have for them. If there is no one that comes to mind, perhaps you may imagine another concept or entity for which you could feel deep love and connection. Take this moment to really feel the love and connection you feel with this person or entity. Imagine yourself being able to share the feeling of this love to that person via an embrace, magically blown kisses, or any other means of transmitting all of the love you feel for them in a way that they could feel and immediately recognize. Notice feelings of joy and life you may feel when connecting with this loved one. Now… take another deep meditative breath, slowly inhaling and gently exhaling any tension as you release your breath. Then, recall the love you shared with your loved one and how it made your heart feel full of goodness. Remember how loving them felt and how good you feel with just the thought of them being happy and well. Now, give that same love back to yourself. Allow yourself to bask in the glow of eyes that reflect only love and kindness. Feel how warm and soothing it is to fill your own being with the same deep and unconditional love. The kind of unconditional love that embraces imperfection and sees goodness within you. Hold space for an imperfect human being who is worthy of receiving and capable of giving love. Unconditional love for the self makes space to find peace within the self and with the world around you. Through allowing yourself to feel such love for the self, you open pathways for your own self-love to heal shame.

Some may find this exercise to be quite challenging. If so, that is not unexpected. This is an opportunity to examine what holds you back from being able to embrace yourself as being worthy of love? Note the thoughts/feelings or beliefs that arise when attempting to offer unconditional love to yourself. If they are less than self-affirming, you may benefit from writing them down for further examination and engagement for change. Everyone has had different experiences in life, reared in various homes with differing rules and expectations, and even born with biological differences that influence and shape a person's life experiences. So please resist any impulse to make comparisons to others or expectations that your healing should be any certain way. This is an individual journey.

Exercise: Expression drawing

This is a form of non-verbal journaling. The beauty of this style of journaling is that because it is non-verbal, no one can "read" it but you! This is especially helpful if you do not have privacy in your life and would like an outlet to express your feelings or simply enjoy an alternative to conventional journaling.

Take a sheet of paper or blank journal page and draw a circle. Begin with a few centering breaths to connect with your thoughts/feelings. Within this circle, you are to choose crayons or colored pencils to color your feelings. You are not attempting to draw or illustrate anything; simply use the coloring medium to shade and apply colors that you feel express your experience. For example, if I am feeling particularly upbeat and happy, I may choose to use bright and "cheerful" colors that are applied with smooth shading and pressure onto the page. Whilst in a more agitated state, I may use colors that express the feeling of that state, perhaps something intense or dark in color applied with greater force, making sharp, jagged marks. You are the key to understanding what these shades, lines or squiggles mean. Whatever you feel expresses your emotional experience works for you. Again, you are not drawing or illustrating anything but using coloring to express thoughts/feelings. Only after you feel the coloring is complete, you may take an abstract gaze at what you created and process whatever reflections occur.

Elana

~~~~~~~~

AGE: 35, MARRIED, HASIDIC JEW, BISEXUAL, POLYAMOROUS, KINKY, MOTHER, WOMAN, SEXUAL ASSAULT SURVIVOR

I was raised in a Hasidic Jewish community and was raised with the expectation that eventually I would grow up, marry a nice Jewish man, and have children, whether you like men or women because that's what we do! This is what is expected. However, as a young person, I also explored sexuality and became involved in a relationship when I was quite young with a man before I was fully aware of my boundaries at this time. We dated for a while, and over time he would keep asking me to send him nudes, and I eventually did send him a sexy montage of undress. But after some time, we broke up, and both moved out of state separately for several years. However, after some time, I was living in Los Angeles and coincidentally he did too at the time. I was feeling lonely, a bit horny, and wanted to make out, so I contacted him and invited him over. When he arrived, he immediately insisted that I put on the red top from the photos I sent. Although, I was initially stunned and taken aback, I agreed and requested that we get to making out after I changed into the shirt, since this is what I invited him over to do. He said no and that he wanted more. I did not want to have sex with him and asked him to leave. He refused, and I sharply told him to get out! I felt quite threatened and scared at that moment and knew I needed to get out of this situation immediately. When he tried to thrust his hand beneath my clothing, I told him that I was on my period. He then swore and left. I knew that he would be totally disturbed by ladies during their period because sex at this time is forbidden in Judaism, even with a married partner. Thankfully, he left, but it took some time to get over how traumatizing this was for me. It wasn't immediately obvious to me that still felt unsafe from this experience. For a while, I just didn't want to have sex or anything physical with anyone for a while. I just tried to put it out of my mind and not think about anything to do with what happened to me. I've never been a person who has felt shameful for being a sexual person, but I just didn't want to have penis-in-vagina sex. It wasn't about anything related to feeling impure, but I did find it empowering to be able to say no and to set a limit with access to my body. This boundary was taken away from me, and it felt good to be in control of my body. After needing time to reflect on this experience and heal from the violation, I was able to enjoy sex again. For me, it was important that this be something that I actively chose to do. Thankfully, I was able to recover from the trauma of the assault and went on to find a man with whom I felt safe and that it was okay to be intimate again.

Female sexuality in Judaism is valued, and pleasure is viewed as being an essential part of married life. A wife's pleasure is valued as being as important as that of a man. In fact, a woman is able to divorce a man if he does not sexually satisfy her. However, with respect to homosexuality, it is forbidden for men to have sex with other men, although there is nothing mentioned about women having sex with women. During the Babylonian time, in which the Talmud and other religious texts were written, it was customary for men and women to live largely separate lives, even having separate quarters in the home. Because of this, the men who wrote these edicts had no regular association with women and did not have an awareness of them possibly having sexual relations with each other, resulting in there being no prohibition on the matter. This allows space for female same-sex relationships; however, there would still be the cultural expectation of a heterosexual marriage. I have enjoyed having the ability to have permission to have sexual relationships with other women and have also enjoyed living my life according to my Jewish faith. My husband and I have been able to incorporate aspects of my bisexuality and enjoyment of kink in our life together. We're pretty happy!

CHAPTER FOUR
Enemies of Happiness, Joy, and Great Sex

The emotional experiences of shame, guilt, fear, and trauma/loss impact an individual profoundly when it undermines the gift of sexuality, something that is naturally beautiful, pleasurable, and some may even say holy. How one encounters shame, guilt, fear, trauma, or loss varies from one person to the next. However, there are commonalities in how they affect sexual relationships with the self and others. The purpose of this section is to deconstruct these influences as they are distortions of sex and sexuality in its purest form. To begin this work, it may be helpful to examine some of our most prevalent thoughts related to sex and sexuality, particularly if they are tinged with any feeling that does not feel good or is uncomfortable. Doing this reflection will begin to allow you to gain insight into some of the concepts that have caused unnecessary feelings of shame, guilt, or other negative emotions. It would be helpful to write them down. Why? Because viewing your thoughts on paper rather than simply a concept in your mind allows you to have greater objectivity. Go ahead, try it! If you do not feel ready to do this just yet, simply note the feelings that arise and name them.

Naming your emotions and experiences allows for better regulation. Because, if you are able to identify the nature of the emotional or mental experience you are having, you are also able to choose an intervention that would be most suitable for managing such an experience. Another benefit of writing down your thoughts is that you will be able to see them evolve over time. Change is rarely quick or simple. This is not something that is expected to be quick or simple either. Be patient with yourself and allow yourself to feel whatever arises for you without judgment. For some, this may be a new practice. However, it is fundamental to developing a more loving and open sense of sexuality.

Many people believe that sex and sexuality are holy. Holiness is a connection with something greater than oneself. In surrendering to passion and sexuality, one can connect with themselves, lovers, and potentially God. One of the most universal understandings of God is that of a being who embodies the essence of love. How can you believe that you are a creation of God and not also believe that you are worthy of love? If there is anything that separates you from feeling worthy of love and sexuality, examine it closer and contest it with vigor. It may be necessary to question your religious upbringing and allow for the belief that you, as you are, are entitled to feel love and enjoy the gift of sexuality.

One of the many tragedies of the colonization of native peoples by European invaders was that many cultures that held an open and accepting view of sexuality were destroyed. This includes an understanding of sexuality as being a spectrum of sexual orientation and gender. In some Native American cultures, gender was also understood to be expressed along a spectrum rather than a binary of male or female. People who embodied both aspects of the masculine and feminine may have been referred to as "two spirits." They were often embraced because of this unique perspective. In fact, contrary to what conservative culture warriors will venomously insist, nature does not always make this distinction either. The existence of people with intersex conditions and genetic variances are some examples of gender and sex being more complex and varied than simplistic designations of being male or female.

The intrusion of these reductionistic European values restricted and shamed any sort of sexuality that was not for the procreation of children within the confines of marriage. That's it; anything else is strictly forbidden. Women were enculturated to believe that they were merely vessels for their husband's pleasure or the carriers of their children. Unfortunately, this remains true for some in our modern society. Women exist for far greater purposes than solely their reproductive abilities. This view is not only reductive of half of all humans on this planet but invalidates the fullness of women's potential. Universally, societies that restrict women from realizing their human potential suffer as a result. Throughout patriarchal history, the primary motivation for sexual restrictions was to control women. In this framework, women are viewed as mere property that is key to the preservation of inheritance and fortunes. And as such, their sexuality was to be restricted so the family wealth would be preserved. If you believe that women are far more than property to be managed, you may begin to question the restrictions placed upon female sexuality as compared to those of men.

Could you imagine a legislative entity seriously considering whether men had the right to control their own bodies? Could you imagine a world where the human rights of men were open to a popular vote? Incidentally, this is the current position of a majority of the Supreme Court justices in the United States of America regarding whether the most basic human rights should be afforded to women. If you find this proposition to be inherently offensive, you may wish to liberate yourself of patriarchal restrictions to discover your sexuality.

The act of declaring and inhabiting your sovereignty as a human being is radical in this political climate. Be radical, be brave! Your mental health, emotional well-being, and sexuality require you to be able to live in a way that meets your own human needs and desires. If you find such limiting and dehumanizing beliefs to be a barrier to your ability to enjoy sex and sexuality, then you may wish to revisit how holding onto them affects your sense of well-being as a sexual person? Ultimately, you have to live according to your own values and beliefs. Healing from sexual shame involves mindfully reconstructing your thoughts so that they are in alignment with self-acceptance and love.

What is meant by the words shame, guilt, fear, trauma, or loss? Just to make sure a common language is shared, here are some definitions of these words to give clarity in terms of how they may be used in this text.

Shame: A condition of humiliating disgrace or disrepute. A painful emotion caused by feelings of guilt, regrettable shortcomings, or impropriety. "I am bad."

Guilt: Feelings of deserving blame, especially for real or imagined offenses or from a sense of self-reproach. "I feel bad."

Fear: An unpleasant, often strong emotion caused by anticipation or awareness of danger or threat.

Trauma: An emotional response to terrible or frightening events such as an accident, rape, or natural disaster, or the experience of having the feeling of one's life being threatened, whether that be experienced by the person or witnessed happening to another. Secondary trauma occurs when a person is not the victim of a life-threatening event but is affected by having witnessed this happen to another person. There are also traumas that form through repeated exposure to threats to one's sense of safety. The experience of having traumatic events occur on a regular basis can sometimes result in a person having complex PTSD (post-traumatic stress disorder). Living in a violent environment where threats are frequently encountered can be difficult to work through, especially if a person has not been able to free themselves from living in this stressful environment. Someone having this experience may benefit from working with a mental health professional or supportive group to process and heal. Of course, there are also people who endure or experience horrific things and somehow are able to move forward in their lives without lingering effects. It is important to take care of yourself without judgment or shame for any experiences that have harmed you in any particular way.

Loss: This can take many forms. Loss may refer to the death or abandonment of a partner or other important relationship. Divorce is another experience in which a person may feel loss. The loss is not only of the person whom you once loved and imagined enjoying a much longer future, but of all the dreams you had held in your heart that now will never be. It is not uncommon for the family members of a person who has come out as being transgender to also feel loss in this similar way. It is not uncommon for the family of a transgender person to feel that they are losing a child or sibling because their expectations or hopes for this person are not congruent with how this person has come to know and express themselves. With love and time, such family members may also come to realize that the person they loved is still the same and that their transition is a gift that allows them to be happy and self-assured. A person can also experience loss when important aspects of their identity have changed as well. For a person who has strongly identified with a job or other esteemed position, the loss of a position or title can also usher in the feeling that they have lost some part of themselves. It can be a sense that some valuable thing is lost and can never be retrieved. Loss is the state or feeling of grief when deprived of someone or something of value (Google, Merriam-Webster). If you are struggling with finding space in your life for the religious upbringing that is familiar in foundational ways and the need to also heal from these experiences, you may feel loss for this connection or association as well.

Given that many of society's belief systems regarding sex and sexuality can be quite restrictive, the influence of fear being instilled into the minds of young people regarding sexual explorations is something that can be difficult to eradicate, even when they have reached adulthood, have found socially acceptable partners (heterosexual), and are recognized as being married. This is especially true for people for whom these constructs do not organically align with their natural inclinations or desires.

There exists a myriad of fears that have been institutionally designed to discourage people from examining their sexual interests. In some parts of the country, politicians are so completely obsessed with controlling the personal lives of others that they have made laws that outlaw the mere discussion of sexuality and gender from being presented or even acknowledged in an age-appropriate and educational manner.

This is a form of grooming that is never discussed. These laws act to coerce young children and others into believing that their existence is an abomination and that heterosexuality is the only acceptable choice. If the reverse of this position were presented, it would undoubtedly be met with violence and condemnation. However, heteronormativity and the belief that being heterosexual is the only acceptable or "natural" mode of existence and is thus codified into society without question.

Importantly, this social/political agenda not only harms people who are not cisgendered or heterosexual (cis-het), it has negative consequences for anyone who desires to be a sexual person free of shame. These teachings range from instilling fears of disease/pregnancy without proper or accurate medical information, "abstinence only" sex education, threats of the loss of reputation or value as a potential sexual partner to the damnation of one's soul should they not repent and commit themselves to never straying beyond the confines of what their society, religion, or social standing would dictate. If this sounds familiar, make conscious efforts to nurture compassion for yourself or others who did not choose the country, religion, or society into which they were born. Most importantly, you did not choose the people who raised you. So, with that in mind, be patient, curious, and kind to yourself as you examine fears and restrictive beliefs that you have been groomed to believe.

This deserves reflection, especially given that these beliefs were imposed upon you before you had the language or ability to consider their significance. Be daring enough to question the rules and beliefs under which you make judgments or choices regarding sex/sexuality. You have the human right to determine how you choose to engage your own sexuality. Your body is the only possession that we bring to this world. Therefore, it is solely up to you to decide how you choose to inhabit it. Fear is a tool of social control. When you are socialized with fear, the very act of questioning official authority is often framed as being a shameful and dangerous violation. Understand that this is an action of social control.

Once you realize that the authorities of your socialization have instilled in you fear as an instrument of control, you then have the ability to recognize that you are the one who is ultimately in control of your life, body, and relationships. You can continue to allow fear to make choices for your life, body, and relationships, or you can take ownership of your life and make the decision to live as your authentic self. As you gain the self-confidence to be your full and unapologetic self, you learn to no longer allow repression and social control to steal joy from your existence. This is precisely why purveyors of hate disdain multiculturalism, feminism, and the normalization of variances in gender and sexual orientation. Once the myth of their moral authority is appropriately challenged, their intentional misinformation no longer has the power to control the populace. That is exactly the outcome they fear most.

Shame is a powerful force. It can cause people to behave in harmful and dangerous ways. For some, the shame of being caught doing something that is deemed worthy of reproach is enough to inspire them to act in violent and cruel ways toward the very people they themselves would like to be. Internalized homophobia perverts a person's sense of self so deeply that they cannot see that this is a psychological reaction to their own self-hate. Shame can be dangerous when it is internalized and corrupts a person's sense of self. How many "family values" conservative congressmen have been found in men's bathrooms or hotel suites soliciting sex with male prostitutes? Go ahead and google it! (logotv.com, 2023; globalgrind.com, 2023)

Similarly, the discovery of repugnant behaviors perpetrated by holy men is in no short supply either. It truly is a wonder that despite untold numbers of heinous transgressions, somehow, they successfully convince others of their moral authority. That is the power of denial. To dismantle influences of coercion from the reality of human existence presents a direct challenge to their power to dictate what is acceptable, thus invalidating their powerful hold on society. There is no shortage of regrettable examples of this phenomenon.

If the champions of hate and discrimination were able to fully accept who they are, they could avoid public shaming, embarrassment of their families/spouses, and harm to constituents they were elected to serve. Perhaps, if they were able to heal from internalized homophobia, they wouldn't feel so fervently committed to creating hostile and harmful policies against LGBTQ people? A person who is secure with themselves and their sexuality would not be so zealously committed to concerning themselves with what other people are doing in their bedrooms. They would not feel threatened by the existence of people who are different from themselves, simply living in peace. Shame left unchecked corrodes a person's well-being from the inside out.

It is nearly impossible to fully appreciate others when you are barred from doing the same for yourself. Brene Brown, a scholar of the influences of shame, notes that shame cannot survive empathy and compassion. If we nurture more compassion for ourselves and others, there would be little use for shame. Releasing oneself from feelings of shame allows for greater freedom and lightness of being. When a person is cloaked in hypocritical façades, they are not able to be authentic with themselves or others. This lack of authenticity creates a chasm that prohibits true intimacy and love. Living in such a dissociated state makes it difficult to enjoy genuine connection with others.

When people are in such disconnected ways of being, they are more capable of causing harm to themselves and those around them. Authenticity allows people to feel grounded and secure in who they are. Ideally, a more grounded person finds greater ease in being able to accept people who are different from themselves. The peaceful existence of others who differ from themselves poses no threat when you are secure with yourself. More than ever, compassion and human connection are something that is desperately needed in a society plagued by vitriolic hate.

By embracing and learning about others, one is likely to see more similarities than differences. This is precisely why far-right politicians work to separate people and suppress mutual understanding. It is not arbitrary that people in positions of power are campaigning to eliminate books from libraries and curricula that feature humanizing depictions of people who encompass identities that are not cisgendered, heterosexual, white, and devoutly Christian. If people were to discover connections with whoever is deemed to be "other," they would be less likely to be whipped into hateful frenzies and blindly follow autocrats who thrive on the perpetuation of the status quo of racism, misogyny, and trans/homophobia.

It is consistently demonstrated that when people share proximity and social spaces with others who have differing identities, they also are less likely to hold racist beliefs or intolerance of others (PNAS.org, 2023). The social engineers of hate seek to discourage efforts to promote diversity in educational and other social realms for the very fact that the lies purported to demonize others struggle to be maintained in the face of their blatant untruths in a multicultural environment. When you see a fellow human as being fully human and deserving of life and love as yourself, it becomes grotesque to witness their abuse. You begin to feel hurt when another human is intentionally harmed, regardless of your own identity/cultural affiliation. The ability to have compassion for others is a human virtue and strength of a society.

By instilling sexual shame into society, people are encouraged to yield their autonomy and desires to conform to the expectations of family, friends, and society. This affects everyone regardless of their sexual orientation or gender identity. After many years of instilling self-reproach for having sexual interests, the shaming authority does not need to admonish you for your thoughts or actions. Their pedagogies of shame are perpetuated within your own thoughts and fears, resulting in your own recitation of shaming beliefs and edicts. These harmful messages can have the effect of causing sexual dysfunction and psychological distress.

However, the legacy of shame does not have to be self-perpetuating. You can engage your thoughts, beliefs, and desires to find peace in allowing yourself to be fully human without apology or shame. You are given the agency to determine your own values and ethical decisions. So long as your choices harm no one, you are free to let go of feelings of shame and self-hate for simply being you. Allowing yourself to embrace your sexuality benefits you and everyone around you. If you feel hesitant to relinquish all that you have been taught, that is expected and perfectly natural. Change takes time, and realigning your views and understanding of yourself may take time as well. Lean into self-acceptance. Err on the side of assuming that you are not damaged or despicable for allowing yourself to be a sexual being.

Guilt is another thief of joy. Having feelings of shame and guilt can be formidable barriers to enjoying sex and sexuality. Guilt may be born from many sources, similar to shame. Many people have been negatively affected by religious guilt regarding their experiences and expressions of sexuality. For many, their understanding of sex was limited to being exclusively for reproductive purposes between married men and women. Less puritanical and more progressive perspectives allow the freedom to enjoy sex for pleasure rather than being solely restricted to monogamously married heterosexuals for the purpose of reproduction. Sex-negative teachings often begin by depicting sex as something that is dirty or shameful outside of the confines of marriage. Many are taught to abstain from having sex until they are married.

However, after years of being told NOT to have sex, suddenly it is expected that the inexperienced spouse suddenly has the capability to adequately please their partners and/or themselves. For many, it is difficult to make the shift between virtuously celibate living and becoming a passionate and uninhibited lover. This experience of cognitive dissonance among newly married couples is not uncommon.

In addition to messaging that forbids sex before marriage, there is often a lack of knowledge surrounding the pleasure aspect of sex. If masturbation was viewed as being sinful, how could a person be able to know what pleases them? Without knowledge of what is pleasing, how can an individual be able to communicate this to a partner who may be equally inexperienced? Many people who have had a sheltered upbringing may also have been denied medically accurate sexual health information. In fact, only 22 of 50 states in the US mandate that sexual education be factually and medically accurate (NCSL.org, 2023). That is less than half of the states!

It is no wonder that archaic and potentially harmful information continues to harm generations of people. You have the power to change not only your life but those in your closest circles as well. If this feels familiar, know that you, too, can enjoy pleasurable sex without guilt or shame. Embrace self-love and acceptance. By cultivating this loving practice, you will be able to heal from harmful influences that have alienated you from your sexuality.

Through the engagement of the thought exercises and reflections in this text, you will be able to shift how you understand yourself and sexual desire gradually.

Trauma and abuse can sometimes have insidious effects on the psyche of the abused, particularly if one has experienced sexual abuse. Sadly, sexual abuse happens to both men and women. According to a survey conducted by the Division of Violence Prevention, National Center for Injury Prevention and Control, CDC, an estimated 43.9% of women and 23.4% of men experienced some form of sexual violence during their lifetimes. This includes any form of sexual coercion, unwanted sexual contact, or unwanted sexual experiences (CDC, 2011). This negatively affects a large number of people who have been exposed to potentially traumatic experiences. It is also true that not everyone who has had such experiences will automatically develop a clinical disorder such as PTSD.

However, for some, the trauma of their experiences manifests in difficulty in being able to enjoy sexual experiences and sexuality. It can manifest in physical and psychological ways. Some women experience extreme pain and discomfort with penetration, commonly diagnosed as vaginismus. Healing from trauma can be multilayered. As you work through how you have been affected, you may feel fear or distrust of others. The ability to trust oneself and others is key to being able to experience intimacy freely. Having this trust or sense of safety violated can distort a person's experience of being a sexual being in the world. Emotional trauma and abuse can harm one's psyche and connections to others. Many people who struggle with issues related to sexual trauma may benefit from working with a licensed mental health therapist to address these concerns, especially if you need more support or guidance. The skills in this text are intended to assist but not replace working with a professional if you find it difficult to achieve relief from negative feelings related to sex/sexuality.

Loss is another complication that may hinder one's ability to engage sex and sexuality in the ways that they would like. Loss can take many forms. Some commonly experienced losses could include the death of a partner or loss of one's health or bodily function in some capacity. Loss can be experienced when one's sense of self is diminished by the loss of status or esteem. All of these experiences have the ability to complicate sexuality. Like all losses, it is important to allow oneself to grieve and navigate the full range of emotions that may accompany healing from these experiences. This could range from feelings of anger to sadness to bargaining and despair. Allow whatever feeling you experience to arise, and then respond by soothing these emotional experiences as they occur. Note any themes or specific thoughts that persistently appear so they may be considered with intention rather than continuing to circulate unchecked. Keep breathing. Like your breath, this too will pass.

After engaging in the practice of meditation or mindfulness, you may wish to journal or practice thought-changing exercises if you notice unhelpful thoughts that are intrusive or problematic at times. This will facilitate lasting change in how you conceptualize yourself and sexuality. Be patient with yourself during the process of grieving loss or any other feelings that may arise as you engage the process of healing. Sometimes recovery from losses comes in waves where you may have emerged from a deep depression to being mostly okay only to have yourself experience a similar low again. It will pass. It is true that change is the only constant. Through the process of finding resolution of grieving, you can find peace and acceptance with whatever change you have come to accept.

Reflection questions:

Have you experienced elements of grief/loss, trauma, guilt, fear, or shame regarding any aspect of yourself as a sexual person? What struggles remain with respect to these experiences? Are there beliefs that are hard to change despite understanding them to be harmful?

_____
_____
_____
_____
_____
_____
_____

Which social influences are associated with these experiences? How much of an influence do those social systems have in your current life? If they are not your current beliefs/values, how has letting go of harmful belief structures affected your life?

_____
_____
_____
_____
_____
_____
_____

Are you able to identify problematic thoughts you have been successful in changing? What was helpful? How would you like to advance further?

_____
_____
_____
_____
_____
_____
_____

AGE: 41. DANISH/MEXICAN HERITAGE.
COAST GUARD VETERAN. CISGENDERED.
PANSEXUAL. MAN. RAISED IN RURAL TEXAS

It's not status quo to talk about sex and shame. I think talking about sex is necessary in an intelligent society. That being said, the journey toward fully embracing my sexuality has been a process of gaining self-awareness through time and experience as an adult living on the West Coast in cities like Seattle, Portland, and San Francisco. I was raised in rural Texas by parents who were typical of their time. They raised us with traditional values, and although religion was not strictly forced upon us, Christianity informed their views on sex, gender, and sexuality. There were prescribed ways to be a man or woman, and that heterosexuality was the expected orientation.

Before I fully understood myself as a sexual being, around age eight, I remember enjoying the feeling of dropping my pants and just feel the air as my naked natural self. This was before I even discovered how to masturbate. At the time, this was taken lightly. Dad would see me if he came into my room and jokingly shout, "Look at that naked boy! Put some clothes on," and kind of brush it off. I was too young to know about touching myself, but I just knew there was something more exciting about my body. This was also a time before I knew that I should censor my interests in girls and boys. I would just be entertaining myself by creating poetry out loud about "strawberry girls," naming off fruits, girls, and boys. Whether it was a girl or a boy character in media or books that would be attractive to me, I would just be saying it out and about. I will never forget when I guess it was either too late or loud or just a nuisance for him to hear, but he came over to my room and immediately flipped me over and gave me a whooping on my butt, and that kinda set a tone for when there are these thoughts and you can't just let them out. So I kept those things to myself.

As I got into my preteen years, this curiosity about sex and attraction grew. My first recollection of having any sort of awareness about my sexuality began when I was around the age of ten. I remember my family going to a fitness club that had full amenities, including a pool, shower, and sauna. It was then that I unexpectedly found myself being undeniably attracted to another boy my age who was also a member of this gym. Until then, I was not used to seeing other naked male bodies, or any bodies for that matter. At the time, I was too bashful to be completely naked in front of others, so I ended up changing in a bathroom stall. As I was on my way out of the locker room, I was struck by the image of a boy of similar age who was showering, and I thought, "My goodness!" I liked how his backside curved out, and until then I didn't know a male body could be so beautiful. I noticed how the water was cascading down his body and was in awe of his form and beauty. He was oblivious to me, with his back turned away. And then, as I looked up, I noticed a face that was looking at me. Just over his shoulder was a much older man looking at me mid-suds with this expression on the brow that said, "What the F are YOU looking at!" It made me immediately turn on a heel, exiting the pool area, and didn't go back in for another hour or so to retrieve my stuff. I had not even sorted out what was attractive to me, whether that was with respect to either boys or girls, before that moment. However, suddenly, I was immediately policed about it and reprimanded at that same moment, although it excited me in every way. It was a joyous and potent collection of feelings. So much of my sexuality was experienced before even having sexual intercourse. I didn't lose my virginity until I was twenty.

Growing up, there were many more instances of being admonished as I learned to find a fine balance of being conscious of who I looked at, depending on who they were and for how long. It was through these experiences that shame built up around even looking at all, whether it's a boy at the pool, a girl, or a relative in my family tree. It has taken me some time to be comfortable with sex and sexuality in general. Fortunately, I have been able to travel and live in different places. This allowed me to be in places where people were open to be more of themselves.

Sometimes, people didn't know what to make of me. I was this former military person who was also into theatre, which made me somewhat of an outlier in either group. Working in San Francisco, there were a lot of queer people, but I wasn't comfortable with just introducing myself with my sexuality at a new job with new coworkers. There was a colleague who was freely talking about his sexual exploits and intentionally left an exaggerated pause that was beckoning questions about my own. A part of me was reserved sharing about my own "gay sex" experiences, but it was also validating to be open about my sexual identity and interests.

When it comes to my family in terms of coming out, I've never had that conversation with my parents. My brother dropped a triple bomb on my parents by telling my mom and dad, "I'm gay. I have a boyfriend and am moving out. My boyfriend and our friends are coming by to help me move my stuff." Then, shortly after, my mom calls me and tells me that he's gay! I did come out to my brother, but it was years after he came out. We were able to bond and connect, which was valuable to me. As far as my personal relationships and friendships, I'm completely out about who I am.

Something I would like is for others to understand that what is between the legs of any given person doesn't matter. Whether we approve of people socially or not, people should consider why they are recoiling from the idea of who a person chooses to have relationships that are not exclusively heterosexual? What business is it of yours what someone does between the legs of someone else? It begs the question, when straight cisgendered people have strong feelings about queerness, do you also spend the same energy/time thinking about the genitals of other straight people and their sexual satisfaction? It just seems so strange to me. What others have to say about sexuality should be solely regarding their own or that of their partners and no one else! It is to the betterment of society when you wish for people to be happy and healthy.

CHAPTER FIVE
Conflicting feelings, beliefs, and identities

The chasm between how sex is used to sell or market commodities and how openly it is accepted in society can be quite revealing. Sex is frequently used to sell products from clothing and cars to alcoholic beverages. Yet adult depictions of consensual sex are oftentimes strictly censored. However, violence is depicted much more readily and is not as heavily censored? Given the scourge of violence affecting the daily lives of people in the United States, one may logically conclude that it would be less offensive to depict consensual adults engaging in sexual activities than demonstrations of indiscriminate killing. It is a chilling reflection of our culture that we have become desensitized to the slaughter of fellow human beings but become reflexively uptight or indignant in response to displays of physical intimacy. Why? Would it be worse to see images of people engaging in consensual sexual behaviors rather than killing and maiming others? Despite sexuality being used ubiquitously in modern society, sex is still a taboo topic of discussion.

These taboos serve to demonize what is a natural part of the human experience. This is an unfortunate societal tragedy as it robs people of an aspect of their human dignity and demeans something that, for those who are not asexual, is an elemental part of the human experience. We all desire to be loved and accepted. Not being able to love and accept yourself causes ripples of disgust that soil relationships and connections between people and with the self. So many people have been harmed by being told that their desires are wrong or that they are wrong for having had them. This breeds self-hate and shame.

Shame will tell you that you are not a redeemable person for having desires that may not align within the established confines of authority. Shame will convince you that you are alone and unworthy of the affection you desire. However, these beliefs can be dismantled with loving empathy and awareness of the thoughts you allow to go unchecked. Mindfulness can be helpful to begin noticing thoughts that perpetuate shame. Once these thoughts are recognized, they can be challenged and redesigned to be more self-accepting.

Embracing self-love is the primary element in creating foundational changes to your beliefs. Remember, if you find this hard to do at first, imagine yourself reflecting love and empathy toward another person dear to you who has a similar experience. What would you say to them? How is that different from the thoughts you experience? If you find challenging negative self-reflections to be difficult, engaging the thought record shared earlier in this text is highly recommended. Through regular repeated engagement of this and other cognitive behavioral interventions, research demonstrates these tools to be highly effective in changing stubborn unhelpful thoughts and reflections.

Changing how you think about yourself and the world at large has the effect of changing how you feel in your own skin. Feeling at home with who you are as a person is the greatest freedom that you could possibly gift yourself. The cost is time and dedication to eliminating beliefs that no longer serve you. Additionally, some may also benefit from exploring help from a mental health professional or sex therapist if your independent practice of these skills continues to be a struggle. There is no shame in asking for help! Continuing to live your life in a way that deprives you of joy and self-acceptance would be an injustice to yourself and potentially to those around you. We are all very much interconnected, and how you feel about yourself impacts how you relate to others. If you wish to invite more love and acceptance into your life, it is also essential to be mindful of how you think of others as well. For example, if you are a person who can be (even secretly) judgmental, it would be easy to assume that others are thinking similarly judgmental thoughts about you. When working to eliminate being concerned about what others may think about you, be mindful of not doing the same. Once you shift this way of thinking, you may notice your life feeling more free or less impacted by the opinions and beliefs of others. You ultimately decide to live with authenticity to your own values and beliefs rather than those imposed by societal influences.

As discussed, many people are comfortable seeing a bikini-clad model on a magazine cover or one standing next to a brand-new sports car at an auto show. However, it would not be acceptable to wear revealing clothing in any situation, at whatever place. There are expectations of conduct and dress wherever you go. Each day, your body is being policed by societal expectations. This is especially true for women in most societies. However, it is also notable that people perceived as being male who dress in a feminine manner are also ridiculed and judged on their appearance as well. These examples are based upon paradigms rooted in male supremacy, often referred to as Patriarchy. Like many of the accepted ills of society, this manner of thinking is so pervasive you may have internalized beliefs that support and maintain the suppression of women and femmes. How you clothe yourself may be perceived as an invitation for harassment, shame, or even violence. The structure of patriarchal society faults the person dressed "immodestly" rather than those engaging in harm or violence to another. If this seems justifiable, question what forms that belief.

Embracing your inner slut is to challenge societal expectations and decide for yourself how you choose to dress or express yourself. Ultimately, your life is yours to live. Each of us lives for only a finite amount of time, and upon a lifetime's reflection of experiences, you will regret more of what you failed to do or experience. However, it is unlikely that you would regret taking ownership of your life and choosing to live authentically. Living according to the wishes and standards of others limits how you experience yourself and the world. We all have the debt of living to learn and love as much as possible in our time on this earth. Live life to the fullest by embracing self-acceptance.

Being a slut is not a statement of how many sexual partners you have had. In fact, you may be a slut without having any sexual partners at all! Being a slut is about owning your sexuality without shame or inhibition. The feeling of being a sexually liberated person can be an act of rebellion. For many of us, to do so is to risk labeling and libeling by others. To own your sexuality is to be comfortable in your own skin and to feel open to having the kinds of sex you desire without care for the judgments of others.

So…how to do that? The first step is being aware of the biases that you have internalized throughout your lifetime. Some refer to this practice as decolonization. Use mindfulness to listen to your thoughts and observe emotional reactions to gain insight into oppressive beliefs you may have accepted as being valid and true. As you become more aware of these influences, actively challenge them by making sex-positive statements about yourself and others. Allow yourself to question the intent and effect of harmful messaging you may have internalized. Remember, your thoughts about others are simply reflections of your own inner being. When you notice yourself making critical judgments of yourself or others, take notice and observe the language and tone of the messages your conditioning has led you to believe is true. Notice feelings of discomfort and examine them with self-love and curiosity. How much sex is too much? How much makes you a "slut" or "whore?" This depends on who you ask. To be a virgin is to have never had (presumably heterosexual penetrative) sex. From 0 to how many partners is enough? Is it desirable to have 1,000 sexual experiences with one person rather than the same with 10? That is an individual question to answer. What works for you is the right amount of sex or sexual partners. Go ahead, be a slut!

Good girls and macho men

In our society, what is good for the goose is not necessarily good for the gander. The sexual expectations of men vs. women vary in significant ways. Men are socialized from their early years to be assertive and to seek sexual interactions with various women before "settling down." It would be acceptable for a man to go to a nightclub, flirt with numerous women, and to take many of them home for sexual encounters. This is often encouraged among young men as a symbol of their status and prowess as a sexual being. However, this is not the case for women. Many women are highly conscious of keeping their "number" or "body count" low. For those who may not be familiar with these terms, it is the number of sexual partners a person has had. Unfairly, having a higher number of sexual partners than a male partner could open a woman to being viewed as a slut, whore, dirty, and ultimately unacceptable as "wife material." Conversely, a man who is a virgin is seen as an anomaly and something that one may be ashamed to admit. The burden of sexual roles and expectations denies both sexes the ability to be their most authentic selves.

The good news is that this way of thinking can be challenged and replaced with sex-affirming perspectives. The journey to freeing oneself from the judgments of others involves choosing your own well-being and happiness above societal expectations. This does not absolve someone of having to take responsibility for their behavior, however. Breaking away from societal, familial or religious upbringings can be scary for many people. All of the admonishments and teachings that have been instilled in your consciousness throughout the years may still evoke fear or shame, yet you are also empowered to question and challenge any belief that hinders your ability to fully embrace your sexuality. You must decide which values are important in your life. If there are conflicts between competing beliefs and feelings, this is normal and okay as well.

Change takes time. First, you may just begin by taking inventory of the thoughts and beliefs that hold you in the grip of shame regarding sex and sexuality. Can you recall the first time you were taught to feel ashamed for something related to being a sexual being? Were you sexualized before you even fully understood the intentions of others? Gradually, as you reflect and gain insight into your own thoughts, beliefs, and experiences, your sense of self may be challenged. Embrace the discomfort of having conflicting beliefs and feelings. It is not only okay but an expected and valuable aspect of this transformation. By observing your discomfort, you may be able to better understand the origins of shameful beliefs and evaluate if this is something that you wish to keep or discard? Be patient with yourself. The beliefs that are conflicted for you have been instilled into your psyche before you had full awareness of yourself as a sexual being. This was an injustice that you have the ability to correct. You can decide what is appropriate for your life and what desires you would like to experience. Allowing the fearful judgments of others to dictate your life will leave you feeling cheated.

Purity culture

The mission has not changed from chastity belts to purity rings to the Supreme Court rulings of 2022 denying women the basic right to control their bodies. Their sole function is to control women. But why is the sexuality of women so feared? It is worth noting that patriarchal societies across the globe are the most restrictive of women. It is also worth noting that these same societies are often restrictive or prohibitive of having women being educated. This poses a threat to the structure of male supremacy. When women are given the opportunity to be educated, they open themselves to being capable of making choices that are formed of their own sense of self-determination. When women are educated, they are not bound by ignorance nor dependence on male figures in their lives. They expand their horizons to consider alternate ways of being that allow for freedom from domestic constraints and the possibility of holding power and influence in their communities.

The mere concept of a liberated woman, free to make her own decisions regarding her body, reproductive autonomy, and life choices, is in direct conflict with male supremacy. It disturbs the "natural order" of male supremacy to acknowledge women as being worthy of the same rights and privileges as men. Inherently, this is a human rights violation.

Can you imagine a legislative body making restrictive medical decisions regarding men's bodies? Could you imagine having men having to petition to make decisions that profoundly affect the entirety of their lives and health? Probably not. This is not considered in any society on earth. Yet its pervasive and systemic disenfranchisement is widely accepted by many and presented in popular discourse as if there were legitimate considerations to the contrary. This would not be even posed as a consideration if men were the subjects of this kind of control and domination. If you are unable to control the one thing that each person is given upon birth, then you are not truly free.

The internalization of male supremacy must also be recognized within us all. This applies to women as much as men. Internalized misogyny is something that is not often discussed. Women, too, can be indoctrinated with misogynistic beliefs. Why wouldn't they? Just as it is not possible to be raised in a racist society and not have racist beliefs, it is similarly not possible to live in a society that is rooted in patriarchy and misogyny and not have internalized some of its demeaning and limiting beliefs related to female sexuality. You can see this evidenced by the number of women who support politicians and other pillars of authority who actively work to deny women basic human rights, despite this being inherently against their own interests. They fail to question the origins of their beliefs and belief systems, allowing this scourge of humanity to persist.

Beliefs and practices rooted in male supremacy and internalized misogyny are critical to recognize so you may be better at challenging the negative programming you may have received. Without this awareness, it would be understandable that you may have conflicted feelings and beliefs about what is permissible for you as a sexual person. Many conservative women bristle at the thought of claiming themselves to be feminists. This is an excellent example of internalized misogyny. To be a feminist is to simply believe that women are deserving of the same rights and privileges as men. If you have difficulty claiming this as a belief or identity, examine how you have been indoctrinated with male supremacy.

Men can and should be feminists, too! Living in a society where all members are given agency and freedom builds a stronger community. What a loss would it be to not benefit from the collective talents of the entire community? Denying half of the population equal rights constrains society rather than advancing its true potential. Understandably, deprogramming yourself of these influences takes time. Be patient with yourself in the process of becoming the person that you truly are. Challenging long-held belief systems may be difficult. You may notice some parts of yourself feeling uncomfortable with this discussion. If so, this is an opportunity for growth and change. This journey is an individual one. It would be natural to make comparisons between yourself and your perceptions of what you believe others are experiencing; however, this is fundamentally flawed and distorted. We all have different experiences and influences in our lives that affect us in unique and similar ways. So be kind to yourself!

Some may be familiar with True Love Waits, an organization founded by Lifeway Christian Resources in 1993 that encourages youth of both sexes to make promises to abstain from sexual activity prior to marriage. As a symbol of this commitment made to God, young preteens and teens are encouraged to wear a ring as a reminder of their vow of abstinence. While this may sound innocent at first blush, it unfortunately has had negative effects on a generation of people, and this continues today.

What is so harmful? There is nothing wrong with someone making a choice to abstain from sex before marriage. Sexual autonomy allows the individual freedom to engage in sexual activities or not, as they choose. As long as this decision is made without coercion or manipulation, being celibate could be an empowering choice. However, the message that someone who does not make this choice for themselves is therefore tainted and unworthy of respect and pure love is harmful. It shames people who do not conform to rigidly defined heteronormative relationships. This hurts both straight and queer people alike in various ways.

For many who were raised in conservatively religious households, they were told that sex was dirty, a sin outside of marriage, and held the consequences of making them impure and unworthy of love from God or their communities. Then, when a person does marry, they are expected to suddenly become sexual partners who are free to enjoy their sexuality. Unfortunately, it is not so simple for many people. After years of negative messaging about sex and sexuality, it is difficult for some to allow themselves to freely enjoy their bodies and their partner's without feelings of guilt or discomfort. Having little to no experience with sex, some may feel embarrassed that they are not naturally gifted in bed. They may have also been explicitly forbidden to explore sexual satisfaction with their own bodies, let alone someone else's.

It can take some time to unlearn this kind of negative messaging around sexuality. However, it is possible. This can start with the affirmation that you are worthy of love for just being a human. If beliefs arise that conflict with this affirmation, examine them. Where did they come from? Do I believe that source to be valid? If so, then why? How does holding on to this belief affect my ability to enjoy sex and to feel comfortable with my experiences of sexuality? This line of questioning may seem like heresy, but it is up to you to live your life in a way that feels authentic. The costs of living in any other manner have both emotional and spiritual consequences. The spiritual costs of living in shame have the effect of alienating a person from a deeper connection with themselves and others. If you cannot be honest with yourself about who you are and how you would like to authentically present yourself, every day, you are living a lie. This feels wrong/stressful and causes people to harbor hate for themselves and anyone who reminds them of their true, hidden selves.

There have been so many acts of violence and hate committed by people who were not able to reconcile the struggle between who they secretly know themselves to be and the constant pressure of feeling the need to conform and hide. This internal conflict creates interpersonal turmoil and the feeling of never being quite at ease. This is not love. Question feelings that alienate you from feeling love for your true self. Most religious groups, regardless of sect, have a common belief that God is loving and wants people to love others as well. If the beliefs that hinder your experience of comfort with yourself as a sexual being are not in alignment with unconditional self-love, then perhaps there may be a fundamental contradiction that deserves examination. Making intentional efforts to remove judgment of yourself and others allows greater space for self-acceptance and appreciation. Mindfulness is a tool that can be used to offer a reflection of our judgments of self and others. Notice when your thoughts are critical of yourself or others, then question if that was kind? If not, how could that thought be amended to be more loving and kinder? This exercise is the beginning of changing negative thinking about yourself as a sexual being. It starts with a fundamental belief that you are worthy of love.

Sex positivity

Embracing sex positivity is finding loving acceptance of your desires and needs without judgment or shame. If this is not something that you feel comfortable integrating at this time, take notice of what makes you uncomfortable. Resist the urge to reject things that may initially be uncomfortable. But instead, take notice of this feeling and respond with loving curiosity. Be gentle with yourself as you examine and explore any feelings that may arise during this journey. Be vigilant of thoughts and beliefs that present as an obstacle separating you from self-acceptance.

Cognitive dissonance is the experience of inner conflict when a person holds opposing beliefs or concepts as being true. An example of cognitive dissonance may be in the experience of someone in a long-term relationship where, in the heat of an argument, you may despise something they said or did, but ultimately, you still have love for them and can forgive their flaws. You can be comfortable with some aspects of your sexuality but also fear abandoning belief systems that have been an influence in your life in many significant ways. It is not unexpected that some readers will experience cognitive dissonance at some point in the struggle to find self-acceptance. Challenge yourself to have compassion for parts of yourself that have been made to feel ashamed of who you are as a person. You did not choose the influences that shaped your view of yourself and the world; however, you can examine and change anything that would negate your innate worth and value as a human being in your life now.

Sexuality is a natural part of the human experience. The ability to accept and love yourself as a sexual being is essential to being able to cultivate peace within the self. Loving the whole self without shame welcomes love and acceptance for yourself and affects the lives of everyone you interact with or otherwise influence. We come to this earth wholly deserving of love. This is still an essential part of you despite the difficulties that inevitably come thereafter.

Reflection questions:

Can you identify how you would like to invite more self-love and acceptance in your life, be that for yourself or others? If this is difficult, what makes this so? How can you alter or challenge any obstacle of positive self-regard?

_____
_____
_____
_____
_____
_____
_____
_____
_____

Have you experienced unconditional love in your life? How did that affect your life? If not, what do you imagine it to look or feel like? Be specific.

_____
_____
_____
_____
_____
_____
_____
_____
_____

Do you hold any conflicting beliefs regarding the human right of bodily autonomy and morality? How does this influence your experience of sex/sexuality?

_____
_____
_____
_____
_____
_____
_____
_____
_____

What aspect of yourself are you becoming able to accept with greater ease? What progress have you made with challenging and letting go of harmful beliefs related to yourself as a sexual person?

_____
_____
_____
_____
_____
_____
_____
_____

Marie

AGE: 54, BLACK, CHRISTIAN, WIDOWED, CISGENDERED, KINKY, HETEROSEXUAL WOMAN, THE PREACHER'S WIFE

For twenty-eight years, I loved my husband. We had hard times and arguments like most married people, but at the end of the day, I knew he was my rock, and I was by his side through good times and bad. My father was a deacon, and we were expected to be involved in church functions and events nearly every day of the week. My mother made sure that our clothes and hair were always impeccably presented as we sat in the first pew each Sunday. Needless to say, religion and church were a central part of our lives growing up. I also went on to study at a seminary school as well. Here, I got into a bit of trouble for asking too many questions, but I needed answers. So, to get those answers, I made a point of looking for the source of everything I studied and learned. Being a woman, some people took issue with my challenging of doctrine and scripture. However, this did not bother me as I was truly inspired and filled with faith as a result of my learning. I love being able to teach others and share fellowship. The histories, cultures, and languages upon which the Bible and other Christian doctrines were based upon something I thoroughly knew and understood. Most people take the Bible and its study from a particular text and denomination; however, through my studies, I have been able to study the texts in their original languages of Latin and Greek. Sometimes, the subtle differences in translation can change the meaning of what is being conveyed. This understanding allowed me greater depth and ability to explain the messages that sacred texts contain.

My husband appreciated my knowledge and wasn't threatened by my challenges of meaning and interpretation. Much like my own childhood, in my role as the preacher's wife, I was expected to present myself in a proper manner and was involved in church activities and functions several days of a week. I found enjoyment in taking the role of a woman who holds her husband as the head of the household and spiritual leader of the family. This didn't diminish my role as a woman as my excellence in being a counterpart to him make the both of us happy and satisfied. Unfortunately, after years of being married, my husband died of a heart attack, and I was bereft and alone. So much of my identity and lifestyle was connected to being a prominent member of the church and dedicated wife and mother. By this time, our children were all grown, and I was on my own for the first time in my adult life since we married when I was just freshly graduated from college.

My husband and I always had a good sex life, and sex was never something that I felt needed to be shamed or made to be dirty. But now I was widowed and still a sexual being. I wanted to date and, yes, even have sex. I prayed and consulted with my pastor at the time about my feelings and wanting to be intimate. I questioned the need to wait until I was married again as I was certainly not still a virgin and was well into my adulthood. While I was soul-searching, I also began exploring alternative sexual practices and came upon BDSM. This was something that I was drawn toward but did not initially understand. However, through my exploration, I came to find comfort in being a submissive. I enjoyed having protocol and direction that was given in this context, and it felt familiar. As I mentioned, as a preacher's wife, I was submissive to my husband, and I knew what was expected of me in any scenario. I knew exactly what would be acceptable to wear. I knew where I needed to be and what I needed to do any day of the week, and I missed this structural formality. This kind of structure was comforting to me, and I eventually found myself becoming involved in the kink community. Now, I live with my dominant, and he directs what I wear, what I eat, where I go, etc. I feel safe knowing that I can trust him completely. This lifestyle looks 180 degrees from where I began but is also quite similar. I'm still faithful and love the Lord. Thankfully, I'm very happy in my life now.

CHAPTER SIX
Kink and fetish

For some people, having a fetish, kink, or unconventional desire may make them feel ashamed. They may have internalized that only certain desires are acceptable, particularly if they upend the power dynamics of patriarchally defined heterosexual unions. Kink and fetishes of numerous varieties allow for a greater range of experience and expression that is not typically acknowledged in mainstream society. Because if a male were to exhibit behaviors or sentiments that are associated with femininity, he would be viewed as less than and not worthy of respect. If you were to be a male who willingly surrenders power to another, you are not a real man. This is the heart of how patriarchy and male supremacy hurts men as well.

By not allowing men to experience the full range of emotions and expressions, they are deprived of inhabiting their full humanity. This becomes toxic to men and society at large. To relieve the pressures described, some of these same men enjoy being submissive in kinky ways. It can be deeply satisfying to allow oneself the pleasure of not being in control and to allow another to make decisions and give direction.

For some women, kink and fetish play allows them the ability to explore their inner tendencies toward dominance or submission willingly, as opposed to being subjected to the constraints of gender roles based on a person's genitalia as determined at birth. Remember, sex and gender are distinct aspects of a person's awareness of self. Having the freedom and experience of being able to explore fantasies that are not permissible as a "good" woman is liberating. A male enjoying the experience of submission is free to release responsibility to another and enjoy his desires without regard for gender roles or expectations, which becomes another form of freedom. Being free to explore your own body and sensual needs awakens the ability to fully experience oneself as a sexual being. It allows for feelings of connection with the self and others without restriction or judgment.

Kinky play with dominance ranges from anything that yields power to another to what most think of when they imagine BDSM scenes and beyond. Dynamics of pleasure and pain may be engaged in a kink scene but may also exist in playful vanilla life as well! Kink may also include elements that do not involve pain at all. The exchange of submission and dominance can be created in any number of scenarios. Your imagination is the only limitation. A "scene" is where participants engage in kink play that is consensual, and the boundaries and needs of each person are discussed prior. There are many motivations and interests for some people to explore alternative means of experiencing sensation and pleasure. By allowing yourself to explore what feels good to you physically, emotionally, and sensually, you may discover that your body responds in unexpected ways. Even as a person ages, their bodies change. Wherever you are in your life cycle, be open to learning more about your body and its needs/desires. This is a freedom that is available to us all.

Having the ability to explore and please our bodies, with ourselves or others, is a fundamental part of the human experience. If this is something that you have not previously explored, allow yourself permission to explore the wonder that is the body that you inhabit. This is the one gift that belongs solely to you. How you choose to engage in sensual exploration is completely up to you. Deprogramming yourself of negative sex messaging regarding the "evils of seeking the pleasures of the flesh" may take some time. Wherever you are along this journey, you can give yourself a reprieve from judgment and guilt by allowing yourself the autonomy to explore your own body however it pleases you.

Fetishes are broadly described as being any sexualization of an object or non-genital body part to a degree that becomes an essential element of a sexual experience. For some people, fetishes may have developed through the confluence of sexual pubescence and a typically nonsexual object or activity becoming linked to a sexual experience. There are unlimited ways in which this could occur and how it becomes a sexual fixation for a person. A common example of this could be how a sexually developing person may find themselves intrigued by the undergarments typically worn by someone of the opposite sex and find sexual pleasure by wearing them or imagining themselves in such clothing. For some, this could be a passing interest or exploration. For others, the inclusion of such undergarments could become an integral part of their sexual satisfaction. There is no shame in having fetishes. We are each unique individuals who learn, experience, and develop in differing ways, and at different times in our lives, so it would be difficult to place judgment on ourselves or others with respect to what a person finds sexually arousing. Provided such behaviors involve solely yourself or are engaged with the consent of others involved, there is nothing for which to be ashamed. Shame only deprives you of the ability to live fully.

There is little certainty in the world other than the understanding that someday, you and everyone you know will die. What a shame to not allow yourself to experience the pleasures of existing in your body! This includes enjoying your body as it is right now, with no alterations required. Sexiness only requires imagination and creativity. To deny yourself the freedom to enjoy pleasure could be considered an act of ingratitude for the magnificence that is our bodies. Our human bodies continuously work to support our self-preservation without conscious effort. The human species has been able to utilize our collective knowledge to advance technologies and science, harnessing the potential of our brains and imaginations. Every acknowledgment of the great splendor of our being can be a prayer of thanks for the fleeting privilege of life. Suppose your mind could allow for a divine connection that is pleased by the gratitude for its creation. In that case, you may begin to understand how embracing sex positivity uplifts the entire being beyond solely sexual satisfaction to encompass the well-being of the body, mind, and soul. Please allow this conceptualization of pleasure to become your practice as you let go of thoughts and feelings of shame for simply enjoying your humanity. You are not abnormal and are worthy of self-love and pleasure.

Admittedly, there could be several volumes dedicated to the exploration and description of all things kink and fetish. Unfortunately, this is merely a sliver of what could be said, answered, and explored regarding this topic. You are invited to give yourself permission to explore this and any other curiosities and interests you would like to explore. Embracing your inner slut is giving yourself the freedom to declare sovereignty in your body and sexuality. Reclaiming the word "slut" is also an act of defiance. By extracting shame from the word used to restrict and condemn the sexuality primarily of women, you are liberating yourself to also be a being who enjoys pleasure as they see fit.

Reflection Questions:

Were there any parts of the previous discussion that were difficult to process? What were the topics that evoked feelings of discomfort? What about them provoked feelings of discomfort?

___

Are there any conflicts specifically related to gender roles or expectations? How would you like to live or experience life without such limitations? What can you adjust now to accommodate your ability to live more authentically?

___

What importance do you place on the opinions of others? How much does this influence how you feel about your sexuality? What positive aspects of your sexuality are you able to embrace?

___

Kenyel

AGE: 25. BLACK. GENDERQUEER. SURVIVOR. ACADEMIC. FAT. QUEER. GREW UP POOR

I grew up in Detroit, not the "new" gentrified Detroit, but the hood. I always knew I was different, and other people could tell as well. It just seemed that I shouldn't exist at all. I was into different kinds of music and wore clothes that weren't typical for other femme-presenting people. Preferring a more alternative style, I just didn't have the qualifications of femininity that were expected of me. I was also fat and was constantly made to feel that my body was not desirable. For a while, I tried to fit in, but performing femininity just made me feel like more of an outsider. I felt worse. But eventually, I figured that people were going to hate on me regardless of what I do, so I may as be myself! Not only was I not a stereotypical femme, but I was also fat and smart. I love to read and learn. Although many teachers were not invested in the students, several took an interest in giving me extra assignments and tutoring because they saw my potential and that I wanted to be an achiever. This alienated me from some peers as well. They saw me as a "teacher's pet" and didn't like me because of that.

If that were not enough, I always knew I was attracted to women. At age fourteen, I was out to my family as being bisexual. They didn't have a problem with me being queer or straight but that they preferred if I would choose one or the other, believing that "that's a lot of people and drama." My grandmother even has a childhood friend who is gay, but that doesn't stop people in the family from making ugly remarks about trans and gay people at times. Thankfully, I was able to connect with other queer and Black people online and through social media. Seeing people be themselves out in the world gave me the courage to do the same. Oftentimes in the Black community, people and things that are "other" are routinely rejected, which is quite alienating. It was through connecting with people outside of the neighborhood I grew up in that brought me to not only loving and accepting myself as queer but also becoming pro-Black. It only made sense to embrace all the parts of myself fully. Embracing all of my identities (Black, queer, nonbinary, fat, and poor) made me believe that anything was possible!

I hated being Black as a child because I realized that being Black meant that I had to face a lot of hardships. Sometimes, just being alive and Black is a form of resistance in a society that is structured to uphold oppression.

I had internalized the racism that was reflected to me daily, but through making connections with other proudly Black and successful people, I came to understand that there was nothing wrong with me but that there was something wrong with the world. Despite growing up in a predominantly Black neighborhood and school, I was still bombarded with racism. The schools I attended professed to be pro-Black, but we were constantly told that "the white kids are doing better, they are trying harder." One math teacher would state at the beginning of each class that "You have four options. You will either be dead, go to jail, go to school, or work a dead-end job." That just made everyone want to be less involved in school. Nothing about that was motivating. I could see why many of my peers just gave up and didn't see school as something that was meant for them

My journey of understanding my sexual orientation and gender is something that continues to evolve. When I was younger, I told people that I was bisexual, although I was primarily attracted to women. My friends called me out on that, saying that I was really a lesbian in high school, so I went with that identity for a while. However, I didn't have sex with anyone until I was eighteen. My sexuality is something that has been fluid throughout my life, and I expect that it will continue to do so. My partner and I, to people who don't know us very well, appear to be straight, but what people don't see is who we are internally and with each other. My partner appears to be male but is also genderqueer. They embrace their femininity, and together, sometimes people just don't know what to think of us. We may outwardly appear to be straight, but we are indeed a queer couple. I love when they wear feminine clothing when we go out together. People stare, and I have come to just enjoy being a bright and happy person. I walk down the street like a diamond, just being out in the world as myself.

Although I am proud of who I am and enjoy being genderqueer, it is still something that I'm kind of private about. People tend to want to judge or dismiss your identity if it shifts as you learn more about yourself. Nobody wants to be called a poseur. Although I enjoy presenting in a feminine manner at times, it doesn't take away from my gender not being solely experienced as being female; it is simply more fluidly expansive than that. There are masculine aspects of myself that I thoroughly enjoy as well. Due to a hormonal condition, I naturally have a beard. There are times that I really like having a beard, but I also enjoy skincare and don't really like how plucking and shaving creates dark marks on my skin, so I choose not to have it. Being genderqueer does not necessitate that I only present in an androgynous manner or that I perform any specific gender presentation. My experience of being genderqueer allows for all aspects of myself to be expressed and appreciated.

It is fairly common for many Gen Z people to shy away from publicly "labeling" themselves in terms of sexual orientation. In my life so far, from ages 10-12, I identified as a lesbian and only talked to other girls, then bisexual at age 14, and now I just see myself as queer. Throughout my adolescent years, I was aware of myself as being queer despite never having had sex with anyone. I just wasn't interested in sex at the time. I was more interested in emotional connection. Now I identify as being queer because there is no specific way to be queer. It allows space for my experiences of being attracted to women and gender-diverse people, as well as fluidity in my experience of gender. So queer fits me best, but ultimately, I'm just me.

My experience of sexuality was also conflicted with being targeted for sexual attention from a very early age due to early development. I was a child and not at fault for how my body developed. But because I had breasts and hips at an early age, people would assume or declare that I was "fast." I learned that people wanted to touch my body in ways that they shouldn't have when no one was around. But in public, I was told that I was too fat and not attractive. This was confusing and made me feel bad about my body for a while, but eventually, this changed as well. From the experience of people making assumptions about my gender, sexuality, and who they think I am forced me to examine who I am as a person independent of how others perceive me. This is something that I feel good about because loving who I am in my complete fullness is what gives me joy!

CHAPTER SEVEN
Queerness

There was a time when the psychological community considered people who had sexual orientations that were not exclusively heterosexual as having a mental illness. It was not until 1973 that the American Psychiatric Association removed homosexuality, classified as a sociopathic personality disturbance, from the Diagnostic and Statistical Manual (DSM), the profession's book of criteria detailing the diagnosis of psychiatric disorders (American Journal of Psychiatry, 2002). This reflected the cultural biases of mainstream society at the time.

Despite trends of growing acceptance of queer people, there continues to be the prevalence of this example of denigrating language in popular discourse. Due to the ubiquity of societal influences, it is necessary to be vigilantly aware of thoughts and beliefs that uphold systems actively causing harm in your life. This gradual shifting of awareness results from being mindful of actively changing beliefs or influences whose repression you have been enculturated to uphold. To be a member of any society, to some degree, is to be like a fish that does not realize that it is wet. Your culture and its structures of acculturation shape how you see yourself and the world.

The practice of mindfulness opens the doorway to other perspectives and conceptualizations that heal the wounds of sexual shame. Adopting the practices discussed in this text will be especially helpful for people recovering from religious trauma. The pervasiveness of culture is that it shapes how we understand the world we live in and, ultimately, ourselves. This inherently has limitations. We are all human. Cultures around the world have made notable achievements in many different aspects of civilizations throughout human history. However, despite the evolution of culture and knowledge throughout millennia, no singular culture has solved all the ills of life or has found the answer to cure the world of its untold amounts of suffering. Therefore, there inevitably exist limitations in how you may have been enculturated to see the world.

Self-actualization is the human interest in being able to evolve throughout a lifetime. To remain in the same mindset of your youth in your later years would seem immature because of the expectation that a person will learn and grow throughout their years, which informs their beliefs and behaviors. Without growth and learning, there is stagnation and intellectual neglect. Your exploration of this book is an example of how you are exploring aspects of life that may not have been presented in your cultural upbringing. This is not a repudiation of the culture that influenced your worldview but simply an acknowledgment that all cultural frameworks have limitations.

Many LGBTQ people raised in conservative religious communities may both believe in the religion in which they were raised but also understand that who they are is in opposition to the teachings of their religious group. The tension of these conflicting realities can be quite stressful to resolve. But it is possible to do just that. It is possible to find peace between self-acceptance and deciding if/how the background that has influenced your life and the celebration of yourself as a sexual human can coexist? Whatever works for you is best. Know that this process of change takes time and a great deal of patience. The beliefs you may have internalized have been repeated numerous times and by many people in your life. It will take some time to practice unlearning messages of self-hate and shame. By regularly engaging in the thought exercises shared in this text, you will notice a change in how you think/feel. The key word is REGULARLY! The fact of the matter is that the problematic thoughts you have created and repeated countless times are so engrained into how you think, that to change this pattern involves literally forming new neuronal connections in your brain! (Sciencedaily.com, 2019) That is no small task and will also take some time. Be patient with yourself in the process.

Because these unhelpful thoughts are so frequently generated, it will take conscious repetition to change this patterned way of thinking. Like any skill, the more you practice, the better you will become until it transforms into a new way of being that also becomes as effortless as the thoughts you experience now. With regular practice of cognitive behavioral skills that reconstruct negative self-reflections, your thinking regarding whatever hinders you now will change. This isn't frivolous pep-talk. The practice of examining and reconstructing unhelpful thoughts has been researched and practiced by countless mental health professionals with clients and has been shown to be an effective treatment approach (cognitive behavioral therapy—CBT) (NIH.gov, 2018). Our brains are malleable, meaning that just because you have thought a particular in a way does not mean that you are unable to change that perspective. In time, your inner language shifts and begins to reflect self-acceptance and joy. The key is to not be discouraged by any difficulty you may experience during the process.

Gender roles are another complication of sexuality for some as well. What makes a man a real man? What makes a woman wife material? Take note of what comes to mind. What if you are a man who doesn't feel the desire to always be in charge? What if you are a woman with a high libido? Would you lose the respect of those you care about if they knew the real you? Some have been raised to believe in strict gender roles that dictate exactly how a man or woman is supposed to behave. This can cause conflict with self-acceptance if this is not your true nature. You can be a heterosexual cisgendered male and still enjoy wearing women's clothes. Cisgendered is to be a person whose biological sex and their internal experience of gender are congruent. Gender is a spectrum which allows for some people to be born with the biological characteristics of a particular sex but have an internal experience of themselves that is not in alignment with their external appearance.

Our understanding of neuroscience and consciousness continues to evolve. We now know that genetically, humans share 99.9 percent of the same DNA regardless of where they exist across the globe. The 0.1% of differences account for individual variances such as appearance and health differences. It is quite possible that as we continue to discover more about the human genome, we will better understand how our genetic makeup influences our experiences of gender and the development of biological sex. My hope is that such knowledge would serve to support the understanding and appreciation of people who may or may not appear dissimilar to how we see ourselves. However, for those whose gender exists outside of binary classifications, you don't need a scientific study to affirm how you knew yourself to be something different from the societal expectations of a person assigned to your specific sex. For many of us, we knew that our biological sex was not the same as how we understand ourselves. We simply did not have the words to describe such experiences until dialogues regarding gender and sexuality began to enter mainstream conversations.

Gender is a social construct that determines which traits are characteristically male or female and can vary according to a person's cultural group. As discussed, gender can be understood as a spectrum of experiences ranging from being exclusively cisgender male or female to the many shades of gender in between. Some may even feel disconnected from gender altogether and feel that the description "agender" or "nonbinary" best fits their lived experience. Biology determines a person's sex but does not always indicate how a person experiences their gender. It is likely that gender identity and sexual orientation are biological traits similar to hair and eye color. Robert Sapolsky, a Stanford professor of biology, asserts that neuroimaging studies of the brains of transgender adults suggest they may have brain structures more similar to their gender identity than to their biological sex. Research continues to explore the significance of these findings further (Mayer & McHugh, 2016). Gender is an understanding of oneself being more masculine or feminine in how they think, feel, and experience sexual desire, as well as how these experiences may or may not be expressed in their outward presentation. It is not necessary to present in an androgynous manner to be genderqueer, for example. Gender fluidity allows a person space to express themselves as they see fit. This may sway from more masculine to feminine presentations. Choose to embrace yourself. Freeing yourself and your partner from gender roles could be an awakening to appreciating the true self. If conflict remains, closely examine what arises. Where did you learn this belief/thought? Why do you believe this to be true? Do you still believe the sources of this information to be 100 percent accurate? If not, then what aspects seem somewhat untrue to you?

The Genderbread image is one that is frequently used to demonstrate the diversity that exists within people of various sexual orientations and genders. Many people from younger generations are more inclined to shy away from "labeling" themselves and prefer to have a more fluid view of identity. This is perfectly fine. Some older readers may also be able to identify with the experience of understanding yourself in terms of cultural frameworks and, throughout the years, come to find a divergent yet authentic understanding of themselves as they age and are less concerned with the opinions of others. As they become increasingly aware of the limitations of their mortality, many are inspired with motivation to live life for themselves after decades of conforming to familial/societal expectations.

Having a vocabulary that accurately describes your experiences can be empowering. To be able to confidently state who you are and describe yourself to others is to live fully and authentically. This does not mean that if you choose to describe yourself with any particular identification you are limited for the rest of your life to always experience the same identity. Quite the opposite! The beauty of having such a diverse array of descriptions of human experience is that you can utilize language to express your experience in whatever manner feels best for you. Be proud of who you are and allow others to fully see you as well. By doing so, you reclaim your own power of narrative. Using words that describe your experiences can allow you to fully inhabit the world as a sex-positive being.

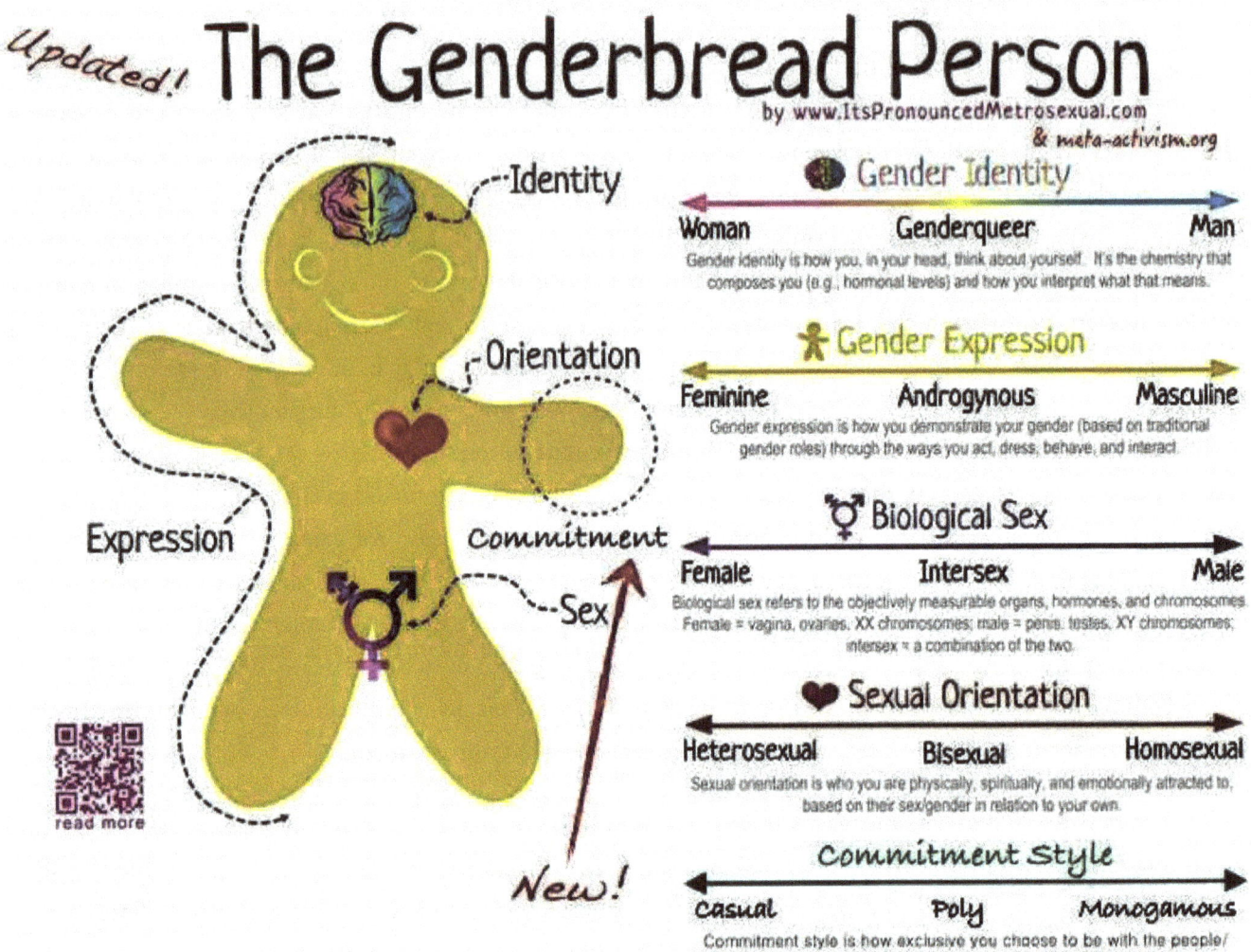

Taken from: www.itspronouncedmetrosexual.com

The threat of "loose" women

Why is female sexuality feared? Female sexuality has historically and continues to be feared by those who support male supremacy. The natural response to the rise of women actualizing their human potential is to control and limit them. We have seen the atrocious effects of this belief system as people with female bodies are stripped of their right to bodily autonomy and access to appropriate medical care. In this worldview, women are objects that exist for the pleasure of men and for reproduction purposes, not deserving of the same respect or privilege given to men. This dehumanizing perspective reduces women to simply being subjugated vessels, not human beings with an inherent right to independently make decisions regarding their bodies and lives. You must look no further than the overturning of Roe v. Wade protections to see this belief system in action.

A country that boasts to the world about being leaders in ideals such as freedom and human rights is also the same that denies half of its population the right to determine what happens to their bodies in the most intimate and personal life decision a person can make. Imagine if there was a world where boys were given vasectomies before puberty and were required to prove themselves capable and worthy of becoming a parent before restoring their reproductive rights! This sounds unbelievable, perhaps even laughable, and it would be, if the realities of such disregard for human rights were not upheld in the laws of a nation so boisterously proud of being free.

Make no mistake, this decision and political agenda have no other intent than to oppress women. If people who support Pro-Life movements were genuine in their concern for unborn babies, then they would gladly support maternal/paternal leave because having such support benefits the child and the entire family. If they were truly concerned about the sanctity of life, they would be protesting in the streets to provide all children access to universal healthcare and education. If they believed that life was an inalienable gift from God, they would have no conflict in ending school shootings, at whatever cost. They would view the support of children and their families as being worthy enough to contribute their tax dollars. They would not villainize people needing assistance to raise the children they had no choice in rearing.

Sadly, that is not the America we live in. The intent is to suppress women and silence uppity bitches who dare to resist misogyny. "Be nice"…"Know your place"…"Be sweet" and "Smile!". These casual edicts may have been a part of your upbringing or culture. How you may have been groomed to accept this societal structure may be an element to consider as you work to shed unhelpful thoughts or beliefs related to your experiences of sex and sexuality.

This is likely to elicit emotional responses from some readers. Breathe. Notice what arises and hold space and compassion for yourself and the world in which you were socialized. No one is to blame for the cultural limitations that have been passed from a multitude of generations past to the present. This statement gives the benefit of the doubt that most people were taught by well-meaning parents who passed on what they learned and may not have had the opportunities you have had to explore more loving and self-accepting conceptualizations. However, you do have the opportunity to be conscious about how you choose to embody those beliefs in your life now. What would you like to share with the younger version of yourself that would be helpful in being more comfortable with yourself now?

Reflective Questions:

How difficult is it not to conform? What are some of the benefits of not conforming to the standards of others? What are some of the risks of doing so? What might you regret by continuing to live according to the expectations of others?

_____

How are your relationships affected by unresolved feelings of shame?

_____

When did you realize you were different from others? How have you come to terms with this difference? What aspect of yourself can you embrace despite not being accepted by others?

_____

Soleil

AGE: 28. WHITE/CHINESE. UPPER CLASS. ENGINEER. CISGENDERED. HETEROSEXUAL. CHILD OF AN IMMIGRANT PARENT

Identity has always been a bit complex for me. I grew up in Massachusetts in an affluent community and attended elite private schools. As an only child, I was given every opportunity that I wanted. From the age of six, I enjoyed taking riding lessons and was popular throughout my school years. Peers in my community were mostly white, although there were a few Asian kids in my school. Most of them were adoptees of white parents. My father is white and also grew up in the same community. My mom is Chinese, and they met while attending Northwestern University. My mom's family all live in China and made great sacrifices for her to be able to study in the United States. This is something she impressed upon me as well. Because her family was not particularly wealthy, she felt the need to study incredibly hard to make their sacrifices worthwhile. Through the retelling of her journey to the States and how she managed to support herself while obtaining a doctorate in microbiology, I, too, felt the overwhelming awareness that I had been gifted opportunities that many would only dream of being given. She was not a Tiger Mom, but the expectations were high. I was never punished for not getting straight A's; however, this was simply expected. My father is a pediatric surgeon. His parents were physicians as well. As a kid, people would frequently ask me where I was from and why I looked the way I did. I didn't know how to answer that other than saying my mom is Chinese, my dad is white, and I'm from here. For reasons I didn't come to understand until I was older, once in a while, someone would keep asking me, "But really, where are you really from?" It always seemed like there was suspicion that I didn't really belong or that I was someone who was "other" whereas my friends who lived in the same community and attended the same schools were never questioned about their belonging or origins.

As I grew into being a teenager, I suddenly became taller and started to get more attention from boys and men. This was a change that seemed to happen over the summer between graduating from the lower to the upper school in 9th grade. Before then, I was always a friend but not someone who garnered any romantic interest. At first, this was flattering, and I liked the attention. People started complimenting me on my eyes and my skin, and

I began to embrace being an object of interest. However, this changed when I was attending a dance with my date and was dancing with a group of kids. My date obviously didn't think I heard him over the music that was playing, but I overheard him being asked about being my date. The other kid was going on about how hot "Asian chicks" are and how he would like to bang one just to see what it's like! I was horrified, but my date just laughed in agreement. The way he laughed sickened me. I wanted to leave immediately but didn't want to make things more awkward than they already were for me. Needless to say, we did not continue to date. When I told him why, he apologized profusely, but I couldn't unsee the way he smiled in agreement, and I told him no. This kind of messed me up for a while. Whenever people would flirt with me, I couldn't help but wonder what their intentions were. This did not only happen with stupid boys my age, but it would also sometimes happen with my friend's dad's being too friendly and curious. It just gave me the creeps.

Later, while attending Stanford University, I shared an apartment with a friend who shared that she was a sugar baby and how she was able to attend school and still have money for trips, clothing, and whatever else she wanted. She told me about the men who would spend crazy amounts of cash just to have her available when he wanted a good night out on the town. It seemed too easy, but she really enjoyed it and seemed to be having a good time. At first, I never thought this was something that I could do; however, for one of my friend's dates, her patron requested that she bring a friend as he was hosting a party. Jessica (not her real name) asked me to come along with her and insisted that it would be a good time. This was someone she had been seeing for over a year, and that he was gregarious but a sweetheart. I was initially hesitant but ultimately decided, why not? It could be fun. Her date sent a car to pick us up and brought us to a marina where he was hosting a dinner cruise. When we arrived, there were attendants to take our things and escorted us to private quarters on the boat. Here, we refreshed ourselves with glasses of champagne and then met her date, who was beginning a toast as we joined the gathering. It was a fantastic evening. Everyone I met was interesting and successful. I also noticed that the dates of many attendees were also beautiful young women who were polished and well-educated. We had a lovely evening and were invited to stay the night on the boat; however, I declined and was driven by private car back home.

After arriving back at our place, I was intrigued by the experience of the evening but never expected my life to take such a turn. The next morning, when my roommate returned home, she told me about how several guests inquired about me leaving so soon. I enjoyed their conversation and company as well, but I still had to study for an exam the following day. I'm generally good with physics and math, but I still needed to review the material. She then shared that there was a gentleman who was interested in meeting for a date. What kind of date, I inquired? She shared that he wanted to get to know me better and was interested in potentially affording me an allowance similar to my friend's.

This immediately brought up anxieties about being fetishized, and I was a bit guarded. I shared this with my friend, who offered to arrange a meeting where we could meet. Surprisingly, he was quite charming and funny. I had a great time and accepted his invitation to join him for dinner the following week. When he shared that he was interested in discussing my allowance requests, I told him I would be prepared for this discussion during our next date. When I shared my list of requests, he smiled and told me I should double it. Throughout the next couple of months, we traveled and spent time attending events; however, this eventually faded out. Having the experience of sugaring (a transactional social or dating relationship typically between an older wealthy person and a younger person that can include financial benefits, mentorship, and support), I was given the opportunity to learn so much from this exclusive social circle of powerful people in business and world affairs. This was something that I greatly enjoyed, and I was happy to accept another date when contacted by a man who expressed interest in Chinese culture and that he had business ties to the country. This time, I tripled my requests and was granted access to an oceanside villa whenever I wanted and was expected to meet with him for dinner twice a month and be available for events.

This went on for several years after completing my engineering degree as it allowed me to not only make connections that have led to lucrative positions but also to have a starter fund for projects that I wanted to develop and execute. Although I was treated with nothing but respect, I couldn't help but notice that much of the artwork that was displayed throughout his luxuriously appointed home was Asian-themed. I asked him about his travels and his interest in Asian cultures. I could see his eyes light up when he shared about his childhood spent in the Philippines and their family's travel around Asia on holidays. I instantly understood why he was so interested in giving whatever I requested regardless of expense. However, this time, I didn't feel that I was being used or exploited in this situation because I was the one who set the terms of our relationship, and I felt empowered by the knowing that my identity was being utilized by me for my benefit. I don't doubt that the friendship that developed between us was genuine, but I could also not omit the awareness of how my ethnicity was desired. One of the lasting lessons that I learned from this experience was to know your worth. Some people will not appreciate your value or discredit you because of your appearance but hold your head high and demand even more than you think you will get. You are worth it!

CHAPTER EIGHT
Intersectionality of race, sexual orientation, and gender

Racial identity is a societal construct. There is only one race, the human race. Biologically, we are all 99.9 percent the same. Yet, people in cultures the world over have sought to identify who they are as compared to others. The "other" could be someone of another tribe/race, religious group, gender and/or sexual orientation. Western societies with histories of colonialism tend to view gender as being a binary of male or female, whereas many other cultures have recognized as many as four genders that included people we would now identify as being nonbinary, genderqueer, or transgendered. The number of sexual orientations continues to expand beyond gay or straight. And that is a wonderful thing!

Having an expanded vocabulary of experiences allows one to better conceptualize themselves and others with more clarity. It is nearly impossible to understand something that has no words to describe it. Imagine trying to describe a color without using its name. This is also why representation in the media is also important. This is why conservative politicians are so threatened by children learning that other people and understandings of gender exist. Such political groups will decry such knowledge as an agenda of "grooming." However, it is their own reductionistic views of life they are self-righteously seeking to impose upon impressionable young people. They fervently believe that their religious views are infallible and, therefore, all others who do not share their worldview must be spiritual and moral enemies or inferior.

Before young children have the opportunity to discover who they are as individuals without the influences of authority figures in their lives, they are explicitly told who they are and what they should look and feel like. They are told that to deviate from the binary roles and self-awareness assigned to their sex is to violate the natural order of life, to be an abomination. If this describes your experience, know that the world is full of themes and variations of a million varieties that have evolved throughout millennia of time. You are simply a variation within an infinitely beautiful and splendid universe. Not an aberration but a unique and innately human being. Being able to see oneself in a positive reflection builds self-esteem and awareness.

Some critics will decry that it is a part of the "gay agenda" to confuse and misdirect the youth toward "unnatural" ways of being when, in fact, it is an acceptable social practice to assume all persons are heterosexual unless otherwise stated. The assumption of heteronormativity functions to create a worldview that categorizes any deviation from heterosexuality as being anomalous to human nature rather than an expression of natural variation in the spectrum of human sexuality.

It is not uncommon to hear adults playfully ask younger children if they have a boyfriend or girlfriend, assuming they are destined for heterosexual partnerships. Could you imagine an adult asking a little boy if he has a crush on another little boy? This would be outrageous to some, yet it is perfectly acceptable when a person is assumed to be straight. This conditioning begins at such a young age you may be coerced to believe that you should be heterosexual too. I'll let you in on a big little secret..."The Gay Agenda" is to create a world where all people feel valued, not to change the sexual orientations of others. Being a queer kid, not being able to see positive images of other queer teens and adults makes understanding yourself more difficult. If beauty standards only appreciated European traits, then most of the world would falsely believe that they were not beautiful. This is why representation matters.

Identities can be both visible and invisible. One may be able to correctly guess my racial identity but may not be able to ascertain my religiosity or sexual orientation. I may be casually perceived as being white, but I am from a mixed heritage of various cultures. One of the ugliest aspects of identifying people by categories of race, class, or age is that such distinctions are frequently utilized for the purposes of discrimination or oppression based upon an identity or categorization of a person.

Most people are aware of overt displays of racism, but many are not aware of the covert forms of racism and discrimination that happen daily, microaggressions. Microaggressions can be described as casual expressions whose intent and effect are to express the subordinate nature of the person receiving this insult, often presented in ways that are subtle but pointedly hostile. These small acts serve to invalidate or diminish the worth of the targeted individual, thus reasserting the social order of privilege and dominance. "Even when people acknowledge that they may have made an offensive remark, it is often described as a small slight and that impact is minimized. The recipients of the insult are usually encouraged to "let it go" and "get over it." Such advice, however, is easier said than done and in itself may constitute a microaggression, because it denies the harmful impact and experiential reality of such biases. Indeed, racial microaggressions are often described as banal and minor offenses and as trivial in nature" (Sue, D., 2010).

Macroaggressions are what most non-POC (person of color) people think of when they think of racism. That is, overt violence or hate speech against a particular ethnic group. However, it is more complex than that. Microaggressions are an assault of tiny cuts that aim to undermine a person's sense of worth. It is a perpetual assumption of being less than, be it in terms of education, capability, or any other measure of worth. It is obvious when someone is making threats to another's personal and bodily safety, but it is equally important to recognize when more subtle forms of racism are being engaged in everyday life. The cumulative impact of these aggressions makes ordinary life daunting. The burden of having to be on guard against the many indignities that may occur on any given day is exhausting!

Sometimes, microaggressions are a result of unrecognized bias but are often done in a manner to express that a person is not of the status of the dominant group. If you are a POC, can you work to free yourself of negative stereotypes and assumptions that are made about you based on your race or ethnicity? What stereotypes have you adopted about people from your own racial background and of those who are not members of your identity group? What does your culture say about people whose identities are not valued? It is important to examine our beliefs and their origins to gain better insight when you are living in a society that has racism embedded into the fabric of nearly every aspect of the culture. This is especially true for well-meaning white people who wish to be a part of the solution and want to end the perpetuation of racism and oppression.

Racism in society is so pervasive that members of an oppressed community can also begin to believe the negative stereotypes that are made about people who share the same identity. Now, consider if you could also shed the vestiges of shame that this same society casts upon people in general, and people of color in particular, related to experiences of sex and sexuality? It is often presumed that POCs are more promiscuous and incapable of managing their sexuality. How often has someone asked how many children I have, assuming that a Black woman probably has several children out of wedlock. How does this and other stereotypes inhibit one from fully exploring oneself sexually in a society full of racist assumptions? It is necessary to decide for the self what is appropriate and desired without the influences of others in order to be comfortable with the self.

Even if you are not able to live openly at the present, it is important to foster self-acceptance by working to embrace yourself as a human worthy of love and desire. To neglect doing so results in a nagging discomfort upon any mention or suggestion of sexuality when it exhibits itself. You may clutch your proverbial pearls at the sight of others engaging in behaviors you would not find acceptable but also not fully understand why such a reaction exists. Look closer at your immediate responses to the sexual expressions of others and how that impacts you. I encourage you to seek opportunities to free yourself from any constriction that does not make you feel good. Work to adopt a sense of curiosity regarding your responses rather than one of judgment. Let go of any feelings of shame regarding who you are as a person. Your value as a human is not diminished or defined by your sexuality. How you treat others and take accountability for your actions determines your worth. A life lived fully has few regrets and rarely laments over the opinions and judgments of others.

When examining the intersection between racial identity and shame surrounding sex and sexuality, one can better understand how layers of oppression exist in society and within individuals. By taking a curious and critical examination of these elements, we can all free ourselves from the bondage of oppression, whether it be self-afflicted or a result of living in a sex-shaming society.

Furthermore, when unpacking the layers of identities and oppressions, one may discover beliefs about themselves or groups to which they belong being less than acceptable. The purpose of this knowledge is to unpack messages of shame and degradation so they may be discarded. The weight of carrying unnecessary shame and guilt for existing as you are as a human becomes crippling and incredibly heavy to endure. Through the practice of shedding these weights, you become more able to feel for yourself and others. With more space in your heart and mind for kindness, there naturally becomes more space for self-acceptance and the feeling of being at peace within the self. Because we live in a society that is steeped in racism and misogyny, it is easy to unconsciously adopt negative beliefs about oneself or others based on popular stereotypes and biased assumptions. Begin wherever you are in your healing journey with the commitment to opening your heart and mind to more love and grace. Each step that you move closer to this goal allows for healing and growth to occur.

One of the tools of oppression adopted by members of marginalized identities is "respectability politics". Respectability politics often adopts the biases of the dominant culture and inflicts judgmental and hurtful actions upon those within the same community who do not adhere to these prescribed standards. It is a form of endogenous oppression often perpetrated by members of the same cultural group. This form of oppression takes values and moral judgments of the dominant class and discriminatorily looks down upon those who do not conform to these beliefs, specifically those who are members of a marginalized identity. Dictionary.com describes this as "a set of beliefs holding that conformity to prescribed mainstream standards of appearance and behavior will protect a person who is part of a marginalized group, especially a Black person, from prejudices and systemic injustices: Black respectability politics embraces the illusion of a level economic playing field. Respectability politics place blame on groups already hindered by discrimination" (Dictionary.com, 1/16/21). In essence, "if you could just be like the dominant group, you would not be the cause of your misfortune; you would be safe from prejudices. However, this is simply not true. Systemic racism and other societal ills also have a deleterious effect on the well-being of people of color, regardless of the compulsion toward assimilation.

Recognizing these societal beliefs and their fallacies is crucial to shedding layers of shame a person may experience. How does your culture view people whose sexual orientation or gender identity does not align with socially accepted norms? When viewing self-acceptance from this cultural lens, how does that impact your own self-reflection? Freeing oneself from the compounding elements of bias and oppression is especially relevant if your identity is not valued across a multitude of social privilege divisions. It is necessary to examine how the intersectionality of identity complicates the path to self-acceptance. To not acknowledge this layer of identity and social consciousness would be to deny an integral part of what makes each of us unique and yet similarly human. Each person's path to healing and self-acceptance is unique to themselves. Therefore, there is the need for patience and grace for the myriad of socializing influences that have complicated your journey of acceptance of yourself as a sexual being. Lean into self-love without concerns of being too self-indulgent or deviant.

Class distinctions are another topic that is not discussed as frequently as race but is just as pervasive in terms of its stratifying influence in American life. Of course, this is not unique to the United States, but for the sake of this writing, it is the place of reference. Wealth and class afford more than just access to resources. They can dictate the literal quality of life and longevity of a person. What does your class dictate in terms of the acceptability of sexuality? How does this influence how you present yourself to others? Do you find the need to live a double life where only certain aspects of yourself are able to be shared with others? How much distress does this cause you? This may work for some. However, others may find greater peace in living authentically. Challenging this may be against the grain of how you were raised, but you may wish to consider the costs of living inauthentically as compared to the benefits of obeying cultural norms but feeling unsatisfied or worse. In certain circumstances, some decide that the costs do not outweigh the benefits. These considerations should include both direct and indirect costs.

In a world full of biases and stereotypes, it is simply not possible to avoid being influenced by such pervasive influences of society. This has the tendency to shape our views of others who do not share similar identities in positive and negative ways. Without conscious awareness, the world has been presented to you through overt and subtle means. Such acculturation influences a person's understanding of others who do not share the same identity. This is implicit bias. It also affects how you view and understand any part of yourself that is not accepted socially. These biases are so integrally embedded in a culture's worldview that it requires conscious awareness to rid yourself of its influence.

This may cause cognitive dissonance between your beliefs and lived experiences. By taking a closer examination of your beliefs and the society that shaped them, you can choose to alter or discard beliefs that no longer serve your well-being. This is not necessarily an all-or-nothing proposition. Within each individual, there is someone who is navigating the interwoven cosmologies of psychology, society, and societal expectations. There is space for gray and uncertainty. Allow this space to exist in your journey toward releasing feelings of shame related to sex/sexuality, gender expression, or any other matter that separates you from unconditional positive self-regard.

What does unconditional positive self-regard even mean, and how do you do that when you have been taught your entire life to reject parts of yourself or feel that your very existence is something for which you need to repent? It is not simple, but it starts with erring on the side of love and compassion. If there is an internal debate that frames yourself as being worthy of shame, then take a quick assessment. Have you harmed anyone? Have any and/or all persons involved in any aspect of your sexuality been given the opportunity for full and informed consent? In such a scenario, it is likely that you have not done anything to which you may reasonably attribute shame. Therefore, in erring on the side of self-acceptance, compassionately allow yourself to connect with an appreciation that reflects positive self-regard. In occasions where this is not wholly true, it would be vital to reflect upon how such violations occurred, how you are accountable, and a commitment to not continuing to harm others. Seeking professional assistance can be helpful when working to change harmful sexual behaviors.

Humans are inherently flawed, yet we possess the ability for growth and change. Your embrace of self-love and freedom from shame is not a singular or linear journey. Each day, you are given opportunities to challenge yourself, lean into the possibility that you are worthy of love, and that how you love and enjoy sexuality is yours to discover and celebrate! What would be some aspect about yourself that you can embrace or accept right now, not just in some far-away imagined ideal state? Change involves a process that requires conscious effort and practice, during which self-assessments may change gradually, and those understandings may be conflicting and dynamic. Amending patterned thinking involves seeking any reconceptualization that is more accepting and loving than the original conceptualization or belief. That's it; just gradually moving toward unconditional selflove and acceptance, one deconstructed thought at a time. The work is not instantly complete. The importance of repeating and internalizing more self-affirming thoughts many, many, many times is key to weakening the strength of patterned negative reflections or experiences.

A curious thing sometimes happens when a person internalizes the bias and hate directed toward their identity. They come to hate the very people who share their identity, whether they realize this or not. This could be a person's internalized racism, homophobia, misogyny, transphobia, or any other stigmatized identity. Unfortunately for some people, their internalized hate causes pain and suffering to themselves and those around them as well. If you find yourself holding negative views or fear of people who share your identity, try to adopt more compassion and empathy for yourself. It is not your fault that society taught you to hate yourself, but it is your responsibility to change this view if you wish to shed vestiges of shame that never should have belonged to you. How much hurt and suffering could be avoided with greater self-acceptance and the release of such shame?

In addition to the countless oppressions and abuses people of marginalized identities have endured, there are also the indignities of being fetishized or characterized as being undesirable. The difference between admiration of someone of another cultural background as opposed to fetishism is that the individual person is not what is seen or sought, simply the identity they embody.

As a Black person, I may not be offended if you compliment my skin tone, but it is another to treat me as an object. An egregious example would be touching someone's hair without permission! This objectification could be the difference between dating an Asian woman or a transwoman because of her personality and shared interests as opposed to simply having the desire to live out sexual fantasies derived from watching pornography. Fetishizing someone's identity reduces the fullness of their humanity.

If you have been guilty of this offense, now you can become more aware and adopt this knowledge in how you treat others. If you are unsure if you have unwittingly fetishized someone, ask yourself if you were acting in a way that advances getting to know someone as an individual, or did you make assumptions regarding their identity that drew your interest or curiosity? If you have been on the receiving end of fetishism, know that your worth extends much deeper than your external identity.

This includes people who may have experienced sexual abuse or misconduct during childhood. A person may have learned from such experiences that their value lies in how they may be sexually desired by another rather than being based upon their intelligence or personal character. Sexualization in childhood fetishized your vulnerability in ways that do not reflect your self-worth. Healing from being the object of fetishization complicates a person's ability to trust the intentions of others. Undoubtedly, this makes having healthy relationships more challenging. The experience of being violated can sometimes affect a person's psyche long after the circumstances that made them vulnerable are no longer a threat. Triggering is when a person may feel the emotions associated with being violated or vulnerable to harm despite the absence of that threat in the present moment.

Stereotypes can be harmless except when they are used to diminish the potential or dignity of any particular individual or social group. Having prejudiced beliefs is one thing, but racism is the power to codify oppression into laws, practices, and other key structures of society. This is systemic racism. It creates a system where all individuals are not given the same privilege or access, and the consequences for the same offense render very different outcomes depending on the identities a person holds. These inequities are sometimes subtle and, at other times, as plain as watching a video of a cop callously murdering a person of color and receiving absolute immunity, complete with full pay, for their crimes. One of the chronic stressors of being a person who embodies a marginalized identity is having the pressure of knowing that should you make one misstep; your entire group identity will be judged rather than being seen as an individual action or that you may suffer long-enduring consequences as a result of not being given the presumption of innocence or access to an equitable system of justice.

It is possible for a person to have both advantageous and discriminatory attributes. An example might be a person of color who is also a doctor. The socioeconomic status of a physician affords a comfortable lifestyle for most. This is an advantage. However, when this same person is pulled over for a traffic stop, their years of dedication and contributions to the community are lost upon an overly aggressive police officer who thinks this individual, due to their skin color, "fits the description of a suspected person" or is innately a threat. This bias clearly is a disadvantage. Considering the intersectionality of marginalized identities and experiences of shame surrounding sex and sexuality, one can understand how living authentically can be enormously challenging. If you are a person who identifies with a marginalized identity, how can you release some layer of oppression? If you are not a person who identifies with a marginalized group, how can you better appreciate how simply being who a person is marginalized by society can be a challenge even without the compounding of shame surrounding sex and sexuality? Be gentle with yourself and others. The journey toward self-acceptance and celebration relies upon the development of compassion and empathy for the self that has been harmed by social influences. Considering the relevance of identity and how that shapes a person's experiences, what part of your experience no longer serves you well? Work toward identifying and making peace with parts that may evoke difficult feelings.

The concept of gender

Gender, as described by the World Health Organization, is made of socially constructed norms of behavior that are associated with masculine or feminine traits. "Gender interacts with but is different from sex, which refers to the different biological and physiological characteristics of females, males, and intersex persons, such as chromosomes, hormones, and reproductive organs. Gender and sex are related to but different from gender identity. Gender identity refers to a person's deeply felt, internal, and individual experience of gender, which may or may not correspond to the person's physiology or designated sex at birth" (who.int, 2023). This acknowledges the diversity that exists among human beings. It views each person's experience of gender as being a part of a gradient spectrum of traits and experiences that extend along a continuum between masculine and feminine.

The experience of one's gender is not confined by binary categories or even biological sex. Intersex people are often viewed as an anomaly rather than a confirmation of the natural variation that exists in the human species.

Consider how your own thoughts about others reflect gender bias. Consider if you have cast judgments upon someone based upon their outward appearance? If you find that you are also guilty of such offenses, this is an opportunity to challenge and change notions of what societal constructs define gender. It is also an opportunity to notice any judgmental thoughts you may have about other people, as this likely reflects something about your thinking that is worthy of further curiosity or consideration.

Take notice of what emotions arise, particularly when they are intense. Is there any association that relates to this experience or way of thinking? These offer opportunities to untangle beliefs that make enjoying sexual pleasure difficult. With loving examination, it becomes easier to find acceptance for who you are, even the parts that no one knows about but you. It is very difficult to both let go of shame and maintain hurtful judgments of others in the same breath. While you are in the process of relating to yourself differently, you may have mixed feelings and cognitive dissonance regarding your adaptation of new beliefs and awareness. This is to be expected. Rather than feeling anxious about this, view it as confirmation that you are letting go of patterned ways of being. Choose to err on the side of self-love and acceptance when it may have been habitual to perpetuate unhelpful messaging.

What messages have you internalized regarding what it means to be a man or woman? If you feel that neither description best fits you, how else do you convey your identity? There is a myriad of words that describe the gender experiences of people whose self-concept does not fit neatly into the discrete categories of being male or female. Genderqueer, nonbinary, agender, genderfluid, and transgender identities also exist for many people who do not feel that their biological sex and experiences of gender are in alignment. The experience of feeling that your biological sex and gender are congruent is referred to as being cisgendered. Being able to be seen and respected for who you truly are is a gift you can begin to give to yourself, even if no one in your family, community, or faith is able to affirm that for you. These concepts and practices may be difficult to integrate at first but are worth the effort.

Reflection Questions:

When did you first become aware of what was expected of a boy vs. a girl? Did this fit how you saw yourself?

_____
_____
_____
_____

If you were free to love whomever you were attracted to, would it be accepted by others? Do you struggle with this in your life now? What are you able to embrace about yourself in your life as it is now?

_____
_____
_____
_____

If others knew about my sexual desires, would I be accepted? What importance does that have in my life now? How would it feel to live without secrets?

_____
_____
_____
_____

So…what to do with all this information?

By examining the intersectionality of race, sexual orientation, and gender, one can better understand the origin and functions of oppressive belief systems that shape a person's life experiences. It allows a person to consciously understand foundational structures that affect their self-concept and holistic well-being. The term intersectionality was first coined by Kimberle Crenshaw in 1989 to describe how the intersections of racism and sexism affect Black women. Moya Bailey further expressed the specific discrimination that is directed specifically toward Black women as "misogynoir" (Bailey & Mobley, 2019). Since the inception of the term intersectionality, it has since expanded to include various identities of people targeted for discrimination and marginalization. "Intersectionality describes overlapping or interdependent systems of discrimination related to age, disability, ethnicity, gender, geographic location, sex, socioeconomic status, sexuality, etc." (Gendered Innovations, 2023).

With respect to the difficulties one may face when grappling with discomfort surrounding sex and sexuality, this psychosocial distress is oftentimes compounded by the discrimination and oppression experienced by people who embody marginalized identities in addition to their internal struggles. Thus, for such an individual, bearing the baggage of a sex-shaming culture and also facing daily aggressions of countless varieties for simply existing makes everyday life much more exhausting.

You may remember believing something someone told you as a child that you later learned to be untrue as an adult. Once you learned information that discredited the previous information, you had the experience of growth and evolving awareness to form more accurate beliefs. Your beliefs and perspectives can similarly change. Nothing is absolute. It is also possible to create space for nuance without absolute certainty. You can be a work in progress. You are not destined only be what you have previously been. We have the gift of intellectual curiosity to discover and integrate knowledge through conscious processing and consideration.

Can you find the compassion to relieve yourself of additional self-inflicted injury by holding on to shaming beliefs and ideals? You may not be able to prevent receiving maltreatment from others, but you are able to create more loving and kind treatment of yourself through how you engage your inner voice and how you navigate all kinds of relationships. When you examine the most salient influences in your life, how has sex shaming, in addition to any number of other biases, made self-acceptance a struggle? Challenge yourself to be more aware of the intersectionality of race, gender, and sexuality when examining your own beliefs and their origins. Are there beliefs that no longer serve your well-being? You can choose not to allow these elements to take up space in your mind and in your sex life with dedicated practice. Building a network of support can also be helpful in the process. This could include connecting with online support groups, local community associations, or social groups. If those do not seem immediately accessible to you, begin with allowing yourself to foster self-acceptance in expanded ways. Your own self-concept is a private domain. This is the space that you can claim for yourself regardless of where you are in the journey of letting go of sexual shame. If you have no privacy, no allies in your community, or freedom of outward expression, your thoughts are available for you to begin creating the change you would like to experience in your life.

Reflection Questions:

Were the intersections of race, sexual identity, and gender something you had previously considered? Were there moments of discomfort or curiosity when exploring this aspect of social hierarchy and organization?

_____
_____
_____
_____
_____
_____
_____
_____

If you are a person who embodies multiple marginalized identities, what layer of oppression would you like to release? Which aspects of shame are interconnected to each of these identities? Are there conflicts among them?

_____
_____
_____
_____
_____
_____
_____
_____
_____
_____
_____

When reflecting on cultural/social intersectionality, can you identify or name the parts of your sexuality that are hard to accept due to how you were socialized in childhood and in your life now?

_____
_____
_____
_____
_____
_____
_____
_____
_____

How does this affect your self-esteem?

Jeremy

AGE: 32, WHITE, SOFTWARE DEVELOPER, MIDDLE CLASS, HETEROSEXUAL, MALE, FATHER, RAISED EVANGELICAL CHRISTIAN

I was raised in Tulsa, Oklahoma, and lived a fairly typical life, going to school, playing sports, and spending time with my friends. There are ten people in our family, including my parents, two sets of twins, two younger brothers, and an older sister. My family are evangelical Christians who were devout about religion, and we had a pretty strict upbringing. Church on Sunday, Bible study every Wednesday, and I played guitar in the church band. I love music, but this was not permitted if it was not Christian in nature or content, so playing in the church band was an outlet to enjoy something that allowed me to have expression in a world where this was not encouraged or tolerated. Don't get me wrong, I love God and still would call myself a Christian, but I don't believe in making it the sole focus of life the way it was for me growing up. In their view, if every thought was not in line with the literal interpretation of the Bible, then it was of "the world," the devil, or sin. There were so many things that struck me as wrong. But I knew that I didn't dare question what was taught in church, repeated throughout my childhood at home and with most of my friends who were also a part of the same church community. I attended our church school from K-8th grade but was luckily allowed to attend public high school as the church school only taught those grades. This was the first time I was able to get to know kids who weren't from the same church, race, or religion. This was largely foreign to me at the time. Looking back, my world was so insular and close-knit that I didn't know much about the parts of society that were not a part of my own.

After graduating high school, I knew I wanted to explore more of the world and see what else was undiscovered. Not having a clear direction of what exactly I wanted to do, I thought I could get started by joining the army. Here is where I learned coding languages, computer systems, and I enjoyed being a part of a team. It is also where I was again broadened in my perspective of the world.

So much of what I was taught was framed in absolute terms of good and evil, forbidden and prescribed. Being in the military made this seem immediately simplistic. There are so many considerations that are not black and white, and there are so many situations that would be morally judged entirely differently if just one piece of information was omitted. We trained daily to prepare and develop skills that enable soldiers to take reflexive action and integrate skills to respond to anything that may occur outside of what is expected.

After my time in the military, I was able to find a position at a tech firm that I still work for today. I met my wife when she took a temporary position when another employee was out of the office on an extended leave. I don't know what happened to me the day that she came to my office, but I suddenly couldn't breathe and was struck by the way she carried herself and knew I needed to get to know her. I asked her if she would like to attend a local festival in town, and luckily, she said yes. Three years later, she said yes again.

We've been married for six years now and would like to have children, but we haven't been able to consummate our marriage. My wife and I both had similar backgrounds, which meant that we were expected not to give into the temptations of sex before marriage, as this was a part of our covenant with God. I didn't believe that I would go to hell for having sex, but I also didn't feel compelled to have sex with someone without having a deep emotional connection. It just so happened that this just never happened before meeting my wife. She was raised in a very traditional evangelical home with her father, mother, and three other sisters. In her home, her father was the head of the house and set the expectations for everything from their activities, standards of dress, and regular prayer and church services at church and home. After the family would return from church, it was their practice to have their father give his own sermon and Bible readings for another hour after they got home. This was not questioned and was how things worked for them. Their mother stayed home and prepared home-cooked meals daily. The children were expected to help in the family gardens after school as they strived to keep their bodies pure by growing much of their own food and only buying things they could not provide for themselves. It was impressed upon all the girls the importance of virtue and avoiding any invitation of sin. This meant they were not permitted to wear makeup or go to school dances and naturally were not to think of anything remotely sexual other than pleasing their future husbands for whom they save their virginity and fidelity. Their father didn't allow them to date until they were eighteen-years-old and were expected to live at the family home until they were married.

When we were married, she and I were both excited to be able to share ourselves with each other, but she confessed to feeling a bit nervous. At the time, I thought this was just a normal thing that we would figure out together. But whenever we were getting close to becoming sexually intimate, she would suffer intense anxiety attacks and would be unable to relax enough to allow things to happen. She also would experience pain and tightness that made any sort of penetration impossible. I knew she felt badly that this had been such a difficult thing for her. She would tell me all the time how much she loves me and wants to enjoy sex with me but was not able to work at the time through the exercises her therapist suggested and had become somewhat depressed as a result.

Fortunately, after trying a couple of therapists, she was able to find a sex therapist who helped her process her beliefs and fears relative to the teachings of her religious background. This space allowed her to also process feelings of anger related to her struggle to enjoy sexuality. She still feels hurt that something beautiful has been denied to us because of this influence. I support her, and we have been able to remain committed in our journey through life together. With practice and therapeutic work, we have been able to enjoy sexual touch and stimulation that does not involve penetration, which has been enjoyable to us both. Seeing her feel more relaxed and able to allow herself to experience pleasure has made both of us hopeful that we will be able to enjoy sexuality together without restrictions, but even if that does not happen, I'm happy being able to share my life with someone who is the kindest and loving person I have ever met. She expresses her love to me and our life together in so many ways, and most importantly, I am happy because we get to spend our lives together.

CHAPTER NINE
The Church

A discussion of influences that have had a profound effect on experiences of sex and sexuality would not be complete without addressing how religious organizations have influenced culture and society. References to "The Church" have been made with respect to Christianity. However, this is not the only religious group to have had adverse effects on experiences of sex and sexuality for many. The ubiquity of this experience is quite disheartening. People from various conservative backgrounds indoctrinated with fear or shame-based thinking about sexuality may experience some of the struggles shared within this text.

The history of oppression by Christianity of sexual minorities and others has a long, dark history. During colonial times, the Christian religion was forced upon enslaved and indigenous peoples the world over. With it came restrictive sexual mores that were not native to the cultures of many uncontacted groups. This suppressed a multitudinous number of cultures regarding sexuality and gender. Due to the centuries-long history of colonialism, many people affected may not fully understand how this history is obscured and how it has been used to subjugate their ancestors. This legacy of sexual suppression continues to this day in cultures affected by colonialism. As of June 2023, there are thirty-two countries in Africa that criminalize homosexuality. Four of these countries have the death penalty for the punishable crime of being LGBTQ (BBC.com, 2023; statista.com, 2023). Without this outside influence, many cultures would have been able to maintain their unique practices and traditions that incorporated a more inclusive understanding of sex, gender, and sexual orientation.

However, the power of knowledge is that it opens realms of understanding for things that were previously hidden or misunderstood. You no longer have to be shackled by beliefs that deny your humanity and worthiness of love. By taking a deeper look into the history and cultures that have shaped the society in which you live, you can inform your decision to choose self-love despite cultural biases that would insist otherwise.

Unfortunately for our society, we were not able to benefit from the examples of such cultures that made space for people of various sexual orientations and genders with love and appreciation. The modern church oftentimes does not preach acceptance of oneself with respect to sexuality. In many Evangelical churches, there are fundamentalist prescriptions for how one is to behave sexually. This may work for some and can provide a beautiful framework to experience life and sex with a married heterosexual partner. However, this model may also cause discomfort with one's innate desires and orientation if you are not someone for whom a traditional heterosexual married sex life is amenable. It also limits what may be enjoyed by such a couple. It is entirely possible to have a varied and completely fulfilling married sex life. You are only limited by your creativity and willingness to decide for yourself what is acceptable. This is where you may examine the origins of the beliefs you were taught and decide how you would like to integrate them with your authentic self. If they are incompatible, choose the best of what you were taught to believe (love and kindness, for example), and know that your authentic self is a reflection of God's creation. You can choose to accept yourself as you are and still be a person of faith.

Another tragic sin of the modern church has included the sexual abuse of children. For decades, many churches and religious institutions have chosen to protect known sexual predators within the clergy and church leadership. Sadly, this is an offense that continues to harm unknown numbers of people who were abused by people whom they trusted. Despite decades of credible accusations of abuse, the Catholic Church chose to hide this ugly truth rather than act to protect innocent children.

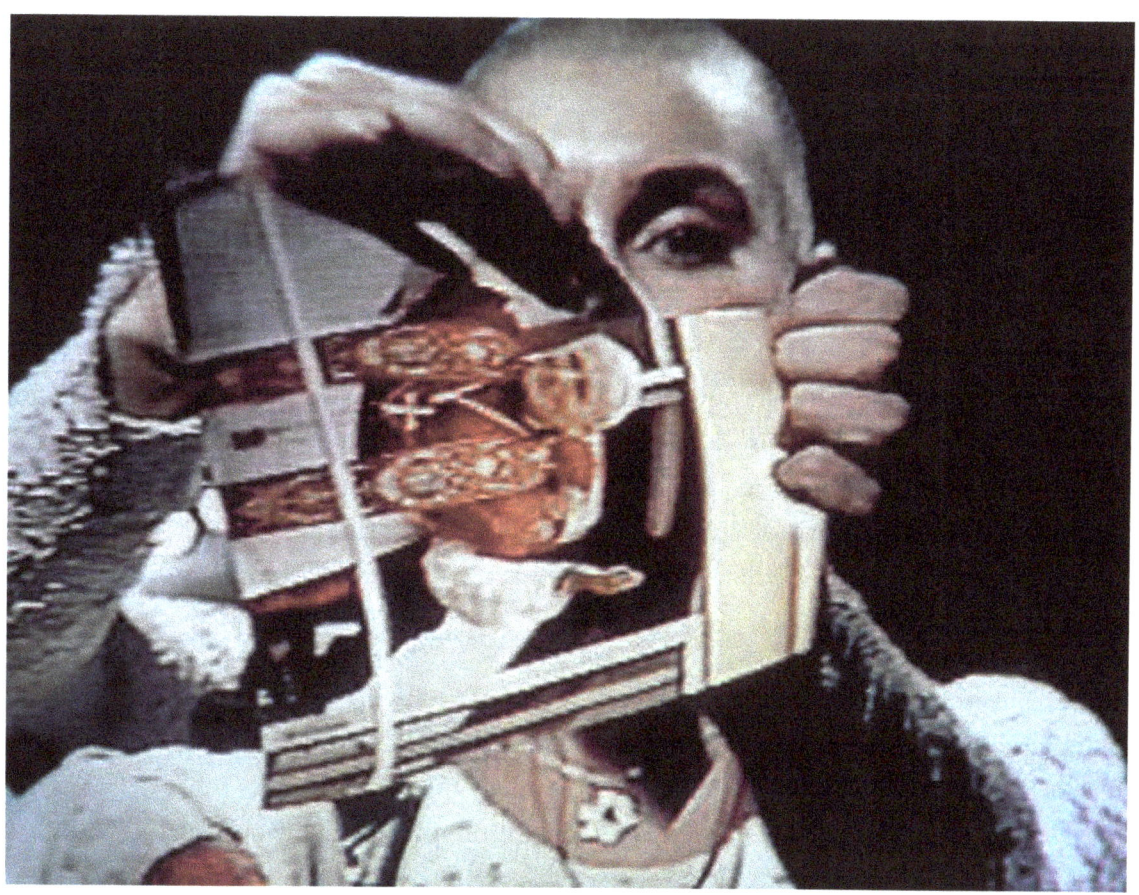

Image of Sinead O'Connor on Saturday Night Live in 1992 ripping a photo of Pope John Paul II in protest of sexual abuses hidden by the Catholic Church for decades. As a result of this act of protest, she received tremendous backlash and damage to her career for many years.

This came to be public knowledge in the 1990s when allegations of sexual abuse by Catholic priests were being uncovered worldwide. After decades of burying this scandal, the Church was finally held accountable for their crimes. Victims were able to seek restitution in the form of individual lawsuits and settlements against the Catholic Church. As of December 2020, according to Bishopaccountability.org as cited by Reuters, the Catholic Church has paid over $3.2 billion dollars in settlements of clergy abuse cases (Reuters, 2020). By no means is this a crime that happens solely in the Catholic Church; unfortunately, it happens in other faiths as well. Experiencing sexual abuse by a religious leader is especially hideous, given the trust that is placed upon leaders of faith. This spiritual injury damages a person's ability to trust and connect with the divine in a manner that should have been nurturing and pure. Violating this trust risks damage to the individual and their connection with spirituality and sex. Many have chosen to leave the church as a result of these experiences.

If you have had such experiences, you may be affected by conflicting messages regarding sex. You may have been made to feel dirty or that the abuse you suffered was somehow your fault. Even if it was not your fault, you may still be made to feel damaged as a result of those who harmed you. However, this was never true. You may have even been punished or not believed when disclosing your experiences of abuse. This is a tool of rape culture used by abusers to keep victims silent. It has a long and storied history kept silent and buried in the hearts and minds throughout countless generations. It has the effect of causing one to question their own worth and value as a human and taints a person's understanding of themselves as sexual beings. You have the ability to release yourself of blame or shame related to your experiences. You can choose compassion for a young person who was groomed to trust a member of the church. Know that you are not responsible for the abuse that you suffered. Your worth is not diminished in any way. The challenge is to release beliefs that perpetuate abuse and to actively work to gain acceptance of who you are, without exception. The path to self-acceptance can be long and hard-fought but is always worth the effort. Allow yourself to grow into the person you would like to be. Be brave in reclaiming your right to sexuality and bodily autonomy.

Another problematic concept promoted by the Christian faith is the model of women being portrayed as being wholly pure mother figures who selflessly nurture those around them, the Madonna. Or they are viewed as being unholy temptresses whose sexuality is demonized and portrayed as the Whore. This paradigm of the Madonna/Whore leaves little room for many women's sexual experiences and expression. It also sexualizes any woman who takes space and dares to not submit to rigid gender roles/expectations. The idealized woman is not a sexual being but one who is servile and obedient. The woman who wantonly owns her sexuality is a pariah, one to be shunned and scorned for her actions and desires.

How can you create greater space for sexuality in the concept of yourself as a sexual being if this has been a part of your upbringing? I invite you to challenge any worldview that reduces your worth to your reproductivity. You have more purpose than simply what you can do for others. While service to others is praiseworthy and something we should all engage in some form or another, it cannot be your only measure of worth.

Being a fully human being involves caring for others and ourselves. As you take the journey toward embracing yourself as a fully sexual being, strive to release yourself from judgment or other tools of oppression. This is especially true for women living in a patriarchal society. Patriarchy posits that women are innately inferior to men and that the man's rightful place is to be masterful and dominant. From this view, women have a lesser role in society and are dictated what is acceptable from a male perspective. Take notice of thoughts that shame your desires and examine them closely. Do they reflect the life that you would like for yourself? Or are they echoes of past opinions and beliefs of others? So long as you are harming no one and obtaining consent, sex and sexuality are human rights you are free to enjoy.

Oftentimes, religion and spirituality are thought of synonymously, but they are not. Religion is a set of beliefs and dogma that is often ritualized in its practice. Spirituality is an understanding that each person and the planet that sustains our lives has value. Spirituality could be the action of seeking connection and understanding of fellow human beings. It could be elaborate or simple in its practice. For many, taking a walk in the woods and feeling connected to the trees and earth is a spiritual experience. Across the globe, through eons of time, humans have created spiritual cosmologies that express the experience of being a part of a greater and interconnected creation. Even atheists can have spiritual experiences! Humanism is a philosophy that centers on the connection of humans rather than the divine. It emphasizes the inherent value of humans and seeks to address human needs with rational approaches.

There is nothing wrong with being a religious, spiritual, or atheistic person. It is not necessary to shed all of your religious beliefs; however, you may need to examine anything that causes you to feel shame about who you are as a sexual being. Cognitive dissonance can be frightening to explore but is necessary for healing from sexual shame. It is possible for opposing beliefs to feel equally true/ valid at the same time; this is cognitive dissonance and is to be expected in this journey. Free will is the ability to accept or decline the choices of others. You can choose to live in alignment with what fits you as an individual.

With this freedom comes an accountability to the choices you make. Being able to embrace and accept yourself fully allows you to be conscious of how you exist in the world. It opens doors of understanding for the self and of others with greater empathy and compassion. Despite the sex negative messaging you may have received, you are worthy of love and the ability to experience sex and sexuality as a human being. It takes courage to be different and to not assimilate to the cultures that surround you. On the surface, it may seem preferable to hide or pretend; however, this internal discomfort can deplete life of its fullness. We were given free will and intellect to use wisely and with care. You are given a finite amount of time in your lifetime to make choices, to learn and grow as a person. It is imperative to also utilize this wisely and with care. Choose love and self-acceptance. This is something you will not regret and is worth the efforts and dedication to your healing.

Sexual and social control

Monogamy was not a common practice in Europe before the Middle Ages. Laws concerning inheritance and the distribution of land and wealth made paternity a crucial concern. Women were regarded largely as property and were not given the same permission to have affairs outside of their marriages. Whereas men, in practical terms, were free to do as they wish. In short, patriarchy. Monogamy is still the social standard for relationships and the idealized imagination of marriage and a milestone event in a person's life, particularly for women (Ziegler et al., 2014).

Thus, enters a society that values virginity and scorns the sexual freedoms of women. This society creates moral codes that venerate the virgin and castigate the "whore." In this Madonna/Whore paradigm, women who engage in having sex outside of the bounds of marriage are automatically whores, sluts, loose women, etc. This creates an unhealthy relationship with sex and sexuality. This debasement of sexuality has the potential to harm both men and women of being able to be healthy sexual beings. It demeans and devalues anyone who chooses to take ownership of their bodies and sexuality. For some of you, this feeling is all too familiar. Perhaps you may be recalling negative messaging you received, whether it was overt to you at the time or not.

Some may have even heard of the analogy of chewed bubble gum being compared to one's body. The premise is that once it has been used by one person, who else would want it? How does this message affect a person whose first sexual experiences were not consensual? How does this reflect the worth of a person who simply wants to enjoy sex with another person? The notion of the ideal woman being a virgin until her wedding day and then suddenly becoming the sexual goddess capable of fulfilling both her partner and herself is not fair or even reasonable. Most people's sexual education conveyed the message that sex was dangerous, potentially causing disease or unwanted pregnancy. Not to mention the grave moral consequences frequently preached to warn those who may be tempted by "the flesh." Many people have not been given accurate information regarding sexuality at all, leaving curious young people to seek this information by watching pornography. Pornography is typically not intended to teach young people how to have healthy and satisfying relationships. Although, recognizing that many curious people do turn to porn to answer sexual questions they have not been able to find elsewhere, PornHub, a popular porn site has added sexual education videos to fill this gap (PornHub.com, 2023. Ideally, there would be the opportunity to learn with greater care and nuance.

The shift from the expectation of virginity to marital sexuality can be confusing and frustrating for many whose sexual awakening was not instantaneous. Rarely does sexual education involve teaching people how to engage in healthy relationships, communication, or consent, let alone pleasure! How different would it have been to have received this as a part of your sexual education? Now is an opportunity to take ownership of your sexuality by giving yourself permission to be a sexual human being in any way that feels good to you. Not receiving sex-positive messaging is a disservice to anyone who wishes to enjoy a happy and satisfying sexual existence. Luckily, you have the power to change your relationship with sex and sexuality by unlearning teachings that cause you to feel ashamed of who you are and your desires. The process of unlearning long-held beliefs takes time; be patient with yourself. Repetition of newly formed thoughts is necessary to replace problematic thoughts that hinder your connection to sensuality and sexuality. When you notice yourself repeating thoughts that no longer serve you, gently remind yourself of your inherent worth and value as a human.

Fast forward a few centuries, and some things have not changed. Women still live under the double standards of sexuality and are punished in varying ways for engaging in non-marital sexual behavior. Do you live under laws that prohibit you from being able to have access to medical care or even birth control because it conflicts with the views of authority figures you did not choose? Have you been afraid to tell anyone about an incident of sexual assault or harassment because you were not sure that you would be believed or could possibly suffer worse consequences for telling the truth? Is your ability as a transgendered or intersex person to receive medical treatments determined by you and your doctor or a politician?

These examples demonstrate how the denial of human rights becomes normalized and enshrined into law and societal practice. It starts with rhetoric describing the (insert scapegoat here) marginalized group du jour as being the root cause of whatever societal element that stokes the greatest amount of fear. Unfortunately, it has the potential to build from fringe rhetoric to being elevated to being worthy of "hearing both sides" of an ethically corrupt argument to even darker turns from there. It aims to separate would-be allies from being able to see the "other" as being fully human and worthy of the same life that they would like for those they love. Meanwhile, while sowing divisions among the people, those who hold absolute power exploit and subjugate the very factions that fail to correctly identify the true cause of degradation within their nation or society.

Knowledge is power. The demystification of forces that have shaped your understanding of who you are and what you should be opens the possibility to discover your innate beauty, power, and worth. Being a fully authentic and actualized self is a state of feeling in alignment with your strengths, with the wisdom to utilize them most effectively and with purpose. Allowing yourself to make choices regarding your own life is your human right, however that looks like for you. Freeing yourself of sexual stigmatization involves examining the origins of beliefs that are codified in your psyche. It is not necessary to abandon all cherished beliefs and traditions. However, I encourage further examination if these beliefs cause you to feel unable to enjoy sexuality freely. Perhaps you may choose not to live according to societal norms based on fear, shame, and patriarchy? This could look like embracing the beautiful parts of your culture or religion but also accepting that some of its beliefs are limiting and based upon the fear of sexuality. By choosing to live free of fear or shame, you can claim ownership of life to discover who you are, delight in the experience of pleasure, and enjoy being fully human.

The enjoyment of pleasure is not inherently wrong. In fact, it has mental, physical, and emotional benefits. When we enjoy the experience of close physical connections with other humans, our brains release oxytocin, a natural hormone that promotes feelings of trust and connection. This intrinsic experience can evoke warm and soft feelings just thinking about the person with whom you have shared this connection. Importantly, this can occur in sexual and nonsexual contexts.

Other neurotransmitters, such as dopamine, norepinephrine, and serotonin are also released in the brain during sex, promoting a reduction in anxiety and an improved sense of well-being (Psychiatrist. com, 2023). These mental and emotional benefits are not trivial. If you have suffered from anxiety or depression, you can attest to how living with a deficiency of these elements negatively affects a person's quality of life. Allowing yourself to enjoy pleasure is to embrace the sweetness of life. Ideally, this would be celebrated and not feared, especially if you are hurting no one and all parties have appropriately consented. Living your life with authenticity offers peace and freedom from the beliefs of others. When you are able to foster and nurture self-love and acceptance, you are free to accept yourself without judgment or shame. This transformation is powerful, creating a sense of peace and contentment with oneself, leaving little room for prioritizing the opinions of others.

Reflection Questions:

What are some of the most prevalent prejudices you notice yourself thinking? How does this affect your capacity for self-acceptance?

_____
_____
_____
_____
_____
_____

How would you like to change these beliefs to be more kind and accepting?

_____
_____
_____
_____
_____
_____

Amara

AGE: 51, BLACK, NEURODIVERGENT, QUEER, DEMISEXUAL, RAPE SURVIVOR, KINKY, POLYAMOROUS, CISGENDERED, WOMAN

Not having representation of queer people in my world growing up, I just didn't have the concept of being attracted to women and female-bodied people. It wasn't until I was in high school that I first became aware of having a crush on a friend, and I was very surprised! We had an intense friendship where sometimes we would be inseparably close and at other times have fevered arguments. But ultimately, we were good friends. Adolescence was a time when I just had so many emotions that it was exhausting. When I realized I had romantic feelings for my friend, I specifically remembered thinking, "Oh! Well, I can't think about that anymore." The societal expectations of heteronormativity were such that I didn't allow myself to conceptualize my identity as being anything other than heterosexual at the time. About a year later, at age sixteen, the first person I told that I was attracted to another woman was my psychiatrist, who was not bothered or scandalized by this admission at all. This was the first time I began to allow myself to think that this was something more than just in my head. This was a novel realization that had never occurred to me before.

As I came into young adulthood, I began to explore my sexuality more. During a Winter break, my brother and I were staying alone at the house while my mother went on a holiday vacation, and I invited my girlfriend over to visit while she was out of town. However, my brother did not react well to becoming aware of my sexuality and seemed to have a lot of feelings about me having sex in the bathtub. He was furious and threatened that "if you don't tell our parents then I will because this is not ok!" So, I did. When talking to my mom about the situation and being attracted to women, I remember saying to her over and over again that, "It's just a phase, trust me..." My mom knew I was attracted to women, and she told me that it is okay to think about such things but that it was definitely not okay to act upon these thoughts! She seemed satisfied with the declaration that this was just a phase and didn't press the matter further.

My parents divorced when I was seven, and they both went to separate churches regularly. Being raised with Christian beliefs and practices, I consider myself to be more Christian than I prefer. It's a complicated relationship to the religion in which I was raised. I have a deep and abiding love for gospel music, which is a conflict for me because there are musical groups like the Winan's where their music is so beautiful, but they are quite homophobic. The journey of finding peace with my religious beliefs and upbringing is somewhat compartmentalized, but I have found a place where I am at peace with myself and my faith. Christianity was a formative part of my childhood, but I felt that what I wanted to do and what I needed to do were two separate things. I ultimately had to do what made sense for me as opposed to adhering to cultural norms. I feel like a Christian in practice due to the enculturation of my childhood. However, my belief is now that God is the kind spirit who is the source of all creation. Within that context, I can still connect with Christianity. Only you get to decide how much your values align with the Patriarchy, misogyny, misogynoir (the intersection of sexism and racism that is specifically directed toward Black women), and homophobia. You have to plot your own course. What works for me and makes me happy, feel safe, and at peace is not guaranteed that would work for anyone else. It is a personal relationship with the divine. I even have a tattoo of an Octavia Butler quote, "All that you touch, you change. All that you change, changes you. The only lasting truth is change. God is change." I carry that awareness in how I relate to the world and with other people.

Another difficult part of my journey of self-love and acceptance was challenged by the experience of being raped when I was sixteen. Before then, I had not had many experiences that were sexual in nature at all. I spent at least a couple of years where I just thought, "Well, that's just how it's supposed to go." I had no concept of what consent was and what it looked like. I felt responsible because I thought I put myself in that situation and that it was something that I wanted. I didn't understand how victim-blaming was embedded in the culture surrounding sexual violence. I still have to talk to myself and tell myself that no matter what I wore or what I said, I am blameless. Being able to understand my worth and ability to set boundaries was crucial in my healing. I'm glad that people are talking about what consent entails and what constitutes an enthusiastic yes.

My wife and I have been married for nearly twenty years. Although we are firmly committed to each other and our partnerships, I love that we are also free to explore relationships that meet our needs in ways that are not dependent upon my partner being the sole person who is able to offer what I need in the ways that I may need connection and fulfillment. We each have the freedom to engage in various kinds of relationships in addition to our own. For us, communication has been what makes our relationships work. We trust each other to be open and honest about our lives together, and it works for us.

The journey of embracing my sexuality and identities has been one of the most impactful aspects of my life. If I were to be able to share with anyone struggling to accept themselves, I would let them know that you deserve to get what you want and need. You are totally worthy! Do not doubt that your people are out there.

CHAPTER TEN
Dismantling rape culture and toxic masculinity

Rape culture is a societal phenomenon where rape and sexual assault is normalized and trivialized through actions such as victim-blaming, sexual objectification, and slut-shaming. These are just a few of the instruments of rape culture that further enable the likelihood and acceptance of sexual violence. By reducing women to objects that are intended for the consumption of men, it becomes easier to permit abuses that coincide with these norms. Because sexual violence is trivialized through jokes and playful banter, those who have been affected by these abuses are reminded that their experiences are fodder for laughter and dismissal. Even more cruelly, many survivors have blamed themselves for the abuses they suffered rather than the person(s) who harmed them and a society structured to be complicit in its violations. It is less often discussed, however, that men experience rape and sexual abuse too. This can be especially difficult for a man to admit, given that the statutes of toxic masculinity dictate that a man is to be impenetrable and not vulnerable to being overpowered by another. Rape is not a sexual act but an act of violence and domination. There is nothing wrong with a raunchy joke or blue humor, in general, but it is important to recognize the impact of words and their power to shape societal norms. By having a broader awareness of how jokes and words can unwittingly hurt those around us, we can consciously work to end rape culture while still maintaining a sense of humor.

It is important to begin recognizing rape culture if you have not been previously aware. It is another salient influence that affects society and individuals. The perpetuation of oppression thrives when those in power seek to cast doubt on the very existence of oppression, let alone the importance of it being a problem of any significance to address. Beginning as early as grade school, there have been dress codes strictly enforced so that girl's bodies are not a "distraction" to boys and teachers.

How is it more permissible for an adult teacher to sexualize a minor-aged student rather than to allow girls to wear shorts on hot days in schools that may or may not have air conditioning? In this model, the female child is held accountable for managing the sexual desires and behaviors of adult men and boys. This is one of many examples of rape culture.

Rape culture exonerates an offender from being responsible for sexual assault if the victim has been drinking and flirting with the assailant. However, if a person says no to a sexual encounter, it is no longer consensual. This is literally rape. It was not until 2019 that Governor Roy Cooper amended a law from 1979 that denied women the ability to revoke consent during a sexual encounter in the state of North Carolina. This means that should she feel unsafe at any point or feel uncomfortable with a sexual partner, she does not have the right to say no after consent was initially given. Imagine not having the ability to say what happens to your body as a result of a law that disregards your right to act to protect your body and mind. Most would feel horrified by this possibility.

This becomes permissible only because rape culture places the blame on the victim rather than the perpetrator. This is often used as a "justifiable" consideration when a trans woman is murdered, especially if she were a sex worker or a person of color. Too often, these crimes go unpunished because all people are not valued the same within the United States justice system. The system that is supposed to blindly view all members of society as equals sadly does not. According to a survey by UCLA, "Transgender people are over four times more likely than cisgender people to experience violent victimization, including rape, sexual assault, and aggravated or simple assault, according to a new study by the Williams Institute at UCLA School of Law" (UCLA, 2022).

How many examples of rape culture can you relate to in your lifetime? Were you told you would look prettier if you smiled and then were expected to respond compliantly, or else you risk being perceived as a bitch? The same is true for catcalling. Most times, this is a crude attempt at flirting. However, sometimes, the consequences of not returning the desired attention are threats of violence or verbal harassment. Have you been told that you are being "too sensitive" when topics surrounding sexual violence or exploitation are casually discussed? Perhaps it is a sense of unease when the validity of a woman's claim of sexual violence is being questioned. Rape myths are frequently used to discredit or deny a person's experience of sexual assault. Another example of this is when people are not safe from being prosecuted for unrelated crimes should they be raped and submit DNA evidence of their assault, as reported by The New York Times (Nytimes.com, 2022). This not only hurts victims of crimes; it discourages others who may be in a similar circumstance from coming forward to report crimes of sexual assault. This practice enables violent perpetrators to victimize people who are not able to speak up for themselves, the most vulnerable in society.

There are many more examples of how our current system perpetuates rape culture and fails to serve victims of crime or to deliver justice. Unfortunately, the life and well-being of a victim of sexual assault is not universally valued. There are states that place greater value on the "parental rights" of the rapist rather than protecting their victims. In the United States, nearly half of the 50 states have no provision for the protection of rape survivors in this scenario. Now that reproductive rights are also being abolished in a disturbing number of states, there is an increased likelihood that a person who someone rapes could be forced to not only go through the physical trauma of childbirth (assuming no complications occur) only then to be further traumatized by having a sexual predator in their lives for the duration of the child's minor years but to also have no legal right to deny this same person who sexually violated you to have access to your child! This dystopian outcome would be outlandish if you were placing it in the context of a "free" and "civil" society. However, it is the reality of nearly half the population who live in such places. This inhumane disregard for the emotional, physical, and spiritual well-being of human life is rape culture as it is practiced in modern life.

Another perversion of rape culture is myths surrounding who is likely to experience sexual assault and who is not. Regrettably, this is something that can happen to anyone. The myth would suggest that a person wearing immodest clothing was "asking for it." In truth, the only person who is culpable for sexual assault is the person who sexually assaults another. Only an enthusiastic "yes" given by someone capable of giving consent is consent. But this myth isn't just reductive; it serves to express doubt regarding the victim's claim of sexual assault. This also creates bias against the victim with judges and juries, resulting in the exoneration of perpetrators and further stigmatization of the person who has been assaulted. These are real-life consequences of the perpetuation of rape myths. Another myth is that if a woman truly did not want sexual contact, she could just fight back or yell stop! And if she does not, then "maybe she wanted it in the first place." In fact, a person who is being assaulted may freeze or dissociate, none of which is consent. Rape culture will frame sexual assault as "unwanted sex" rather than an actual crime.

Such beliefs are not only held by rapists but by many male legislators who make laws regarding whether women have the right to control the autonomy of their own bodies. A fine example of this was when a former Republican senator from Missouri, Todd Akin, said abortions would not be necessary for rape victims because, "If it's legitimate rape, the female body has ways to try to shut the whole thing down" (Time, 2012). These beliefs are dangerous and have deleterious effects on the lives of real people. Now that physicians are not able to act in the best interest of their pregnant patients but are constrained by laws that were not written based on medical advice or research, maternal mortality will increase. The goal of restricting reproductive rights has no concern for the sanctity of life but to violently maintain misogynistic structures of oppression and disenfranchisement.

How many times have you heard the term "child prostitute" rather than sex trafficking victim? When the truth is that such children are oftentimes not making the choice to engage in sex work of their free will but as a result of the many cracks in society that allow for some lives to be valued and not others. Sadly, many homeless youths become targets of sex trafficking. Many times, it is the sexual orientation or gender expression of the youth that makes them vulnerable to being made homeless after being rejected by their caregivers/parents. Approximately 40% of homeless youth identify as LGBTQ, and 46% report being rejected by their families. These youth are 7.4 times more likely to experience acts of sexual violence than their heterosexual peers and are 3 to 7 times more likely to engage in "survival sex." Survival sex is when a person engages in sexual acts to secure housing, food, or other basic needs (Polaris, 2022). In some of the most conservative households, parents would rather lose their children to the streets than accept them for who they are. It may be easier to think that such things happen to other people from places not near my own. However, this is just not true.

How have you internalized rape culture within your own beliefs and prejudices? It's vital to take this examination as it has the ability to undermine beliefs actualizing your inherent worth as an individual. If one were to internalize that they are somehow responsible for being targeted for sexual violence and abuses against them, it would be more challenging to feel that they are worthy of love and respect. If that has been your experience, challenge the beliefs that support viewing people who have experienced sexual assault as being "damaged" or "unclean." Know that your worth is not tied to your experiences of abuse or pleasure. Questioning the status quo can feel dangerous and unsettling at times. This does not mean that it is an investigation that one should ignore. Challenging foundational beliefs that foster self-hate or shame is an opportunity to live life to its fullest. If you were free from beliefs rooted in misogyny, homophobia, transphobia, and rape culture, who would you be instead? Could you imagine yourself feeling comfortable in your own skin? Could you allow yourself to love and enjoy sex in a way that felt good for you, not because society dictated it, but because you felt happy and alive?

Oftentimes, patriarchal authority figures attempt to dissuade others from adopting this belief, warning of great calamity or eternal damnation, simply because they fear women being sovereign entities that can decide their own life choices. These powerful influencers of society aim to control feminine sexuality because it is terrifying.

Women occupying their bodies that crave sexual desire is in direct confrontation with the patriarchy's assertion that men alone should have power and supreme dominance. Permitting women to be unashamed of their sexual needs threatens to destabilize current power structures, allowing them to wield power in realms beyond solely domestic life. Not having control of women undermines this false paradigm and is frightening to those who are invested in perpetuating patriarchal control.

Unfortunately, because of the prevalence of patriarchal influences in modern society, both men and women can adopt misogynist principles and beliefs. If you are a woman who has been taught that men are the supreme decision-makers or that your place is to be subservient and accepting of your lower-class status, you may have adopted patriarchy and misogyny as well. Being steeped in a world that orders society in such ways means that you were taught that this is the right and natural order of things, whether that was explicitly codified or subjectively understood to be. So be patient with yourself, inquisitive of assumptions and beliefs to which you have been exposed and choose to begin challenging and changing these beliefs in favor of self-love and acceptance. Know that your worth and value is a birthright of being a human being. Allowing yourself to be free of beliefs that contradict that basic understanding allows one to embrace one's sexuality, regardless of gender, fully.

No discussion on rape culture would be complete without the glaring omission of teaching boys and men not to rape. So much of the education regarding the prevention of sexual assault is focused on how women can avoid being targets of violence rather than teaching males about consent and neutralizing toxic masculinity. Women are taught self-defense, told to carry mace or another weapon, advised to not be alone after dark rather than instructing males to respect the boundaries of others, and to have the emotional intelligence to know when someone is enjoying a sexual encounter and when they are not. Only consent given freely by a person who has reached the sexual age of consent is acceptable. When in doubt, teach males that it is better to miss out on a sexual experience than to violate someone else. This includes sex with someone who is intoxicated or impaired of the ability to make clear and conscious decisions.

These are topics taught by more progressive countries in an age-appropriate manner, beginning in elementary school and continuing through high school. This allows children to develop emotional intelligence skills, communication skills, and teachings that value males and females equally. This style of teaching would work to dismantle rape culture. We as a society have a collective influence on the generations that follow. Teaching men and boys how not to engage in sexual assault is the solution to ending sexual violence against women. This is not solely a women's issue; it affects everyone. This makes male feminists especially important in shifting the acceptable norms by holding each other accountable.

There are factions of society that believe that men learning and behaving with emotional intelligence are emasculated, rather than appreciating how people of differing genders can have complementary strengths. Men are no less masculine when they utilize their physical strengths for protection or production than men who are naturally better at providing care or creative arts. By allowing each individual to explore and discover their own unique traits and talents, each person is encouraged to develop into their best selves.

Humans are paradoxically more similar than not but also unique and varied across the entire spectrum of humanity. Can you remember having a wish or interest as a small child that was discouraged because of your biological sex? This may have been quite confusing as to why when you were simply curious or expressed interest in something you enjoyed, not having not yet codified such expectations of who you were presumed to be. What would you have liked to have become when you were younger? If gender roles and limitations were absent from your life, what would change? How would it feel to unburden yourself of expectations that do not align with your true self?

Each of us has been influenced and molded by our native cultures and lived experiences. The journey of self-discovery allows you to reconnect with the best of who you are and achieve your full potential. This is self-actualization. It is stunted and thwarted by each restriction that places a barrier between embodying your authentic self and connecting with the best of your humanity. Could history have been altered by Adolf Hitler being admitted to art school? (Grunge.com, 2023) That's another volume of discussion but also an extreme yet relevant example of a tragic collision of toxic masculinity and a person barred from following their passions due to a lack of acceptance from others.

How toxic masculinity hurts men

The unintended harm of patriarchal beliefs and toxic masculinity to men is worth discussing. Toxic masculinity can include traits such as: unconditional physical toughness, physical aggression, fear of emotion, discrimination against people that are not heterosexual, hyper-independence, sexual aggression or violence, and antifeminist behavior (Green Hill, 2022). These harmful influences include the inability to express oneself without fear of being shamed or rejected by other men and society at large.

It is an enormous pressure to be denied the ability to feel what you truly feel or the inability to decline assumed societal expectations that are not authentic to who you are as a person. This is a degradation of a person's humanity at its core. Homo sapiens are a species that is differentiated from other primates by our cognitive and bipedal capabilities. Therefore, the cognitive and sentient aspect of being a human defines our very existence. To deny something so essential to your being as your awareness of self is to strip away your basic humanity. Sadly, this is done from the moment we come to existence in this world. In modern times, this is declared before you were even born. The burden of denying such an elemental part of being a human separates a person from their humanity and humane ways of engaging the world at large.

The cringe-worthy practice of pregnancy "gender reveals" demonstrates how strongly society feels compelled to know the sex (not to be confused with gender) of the child so they can conceptualize what this child will become. This conceptualization will shape your socialization in society. Before you have an opportunity to discover who you are as a human being, social influences such as parents, school, communities, and society will dictate how you should see yourself and your relationships of the self to others in the social group. Noting the differentiation between being born with the sex of male genitalia as compared to female determines an entire life's trajectory of expectations and social conditioning.

Depending on the society in which you were born, this influences nearly every aspect of your life. So, it is not unexpected that being raised in a society that expects you to be cut off from your humanity, toxic behaviors would become normative. Like any false belief or understanding, once you begin to recognize how it harms you and others, you then can alter how you continue to be affected by harmful beliefs that are antagonistic to your well-being. This change begins with you.

Take a moment to think about how you would be the same or different if you were free to express your feelings without feeling ashamed or that your masculinity would be diminished? What aspects of yourself do you feel unable to share with others for fear of being ridiculed? Could you allow yourself to admit that you do not always want to do the things that are expected of men? Would you prefer to be free to make choices that were specific to how you experience the world without the influences of gender roles? What gender roles are hard for you to perform? How do you feel comparing yourself to other men or what society says you should be? Do you find yourself comparing yourself to other men? If so, how and in what ways? How would you like to live instead? Once you have allowed yourself space for introspection on these questions, you may begin to consider how you may have unwittingly or consciously perpetuated harm through actions of toxic masculinity? The purpose of this reflection is not to get stuck feeling bad about yourself or anyone in particular. The purpose is to give you the ability to make different choices. With the confidence you feel in yourself as a result of greater self-acceptance and freedom from the burden of shame, how can you positively influence your life and your communities? How will you inspire others when you free yourself of the yolks of shame and societal expectations? This is the path of healing. Feeling badly about mistakes, regrets, or circumstances beyond your control has little value or utility with respect to your healing from anything that separates you from finding love and appreciation for who you are as a person. What you do to correct such injustices is what matters. How will you adjust how you relate to women and feminine people? How will you confront sexism, transphobia, homophobia, and misogyny when you encounter this toxic behavior from other men? Will you be brave to stand against such ills? If you are a mother raising boys, how will you teach them to become men worthy of respect and admiration while allowing them to develop into the unique beings they are meant to be? This may be difficult if this is not normative within your family or community. However, your conscious intent to not instill the same harms that you are healing from today is an invaluable inheritance that will benefit generations. If you are not able to do that just yet, that's ok. Beginning with yourself and how you relate to the self is a catalyst for change in the world. It begins with you.

Reflection Questions:

When were you first aware of being male or female? How was this experience?

_____
_____
_____
_____
_____
_____

Do you have traits inconsistent with societal expectations of sex or gender? How did you feel when you inadvertently diverged from expected gender roles in your social group?

_____
_____
_____
_____
_____
_____

If you were free of societal expectations of gender, how would you prefer to live differently?

_____
_____
_____
_____
_____
_____

Affirmative sexual education

How much more satisfying relationships would be if people were taught healthy sex and relationship skills? Radically, how might sexuality education be improved if teachings included the experience of pleasure, not just the mechanics of avoiding pregnancy or disease? While these topics are important, there is more to consider in terms of having a healthy sexual relationship. Having effective communication skills facilitates better sex and relationships of all kinds. What would it have been like if your introduction to sex included learning about intimacy and consent?

The good news is that it is not too late to re-educate yourself regarding your inherent right to enjoy your own body and to decide for yourself how you would like to experience your sexuality. If this is new to you, start by offering yourself affirmative thoughts that challenge any negative messaging you may have encountered in the world. Begin with allowing yourself to love your whole being, not just certain parts. For many, this may be a challenge. Start with this wherever you are at this moment and allow self-acceptance and affirmation to integrate into your thoughts and being. This could look like seeking to identify aspects of yourself that are easier to accept or embrace, even if embracing the wholeness of yourself is initially a challenge. Know that through allowing this practice to develop, you will begin to feel differently.

Changes like these are often subtle and then gradually shift toward self-love and acceptance until, at some point, this becomes your dominant narrative. You will start to notice the tone of your inner voice becoming more supportive than critical. Know that with regular practice of cognitive skills discussed in this text you will notice a shift in how you feel as a result of this practice. Rarely do things that are of great importance materialize as swiftly as we would prefer; this will likely begin with intentional effort at first. However, the dedication to your holistic well-being will continue to strengthen as you take the journey from living with shame to self-acceptance.

What is meant by holistic well-being? We humans are comprised of more than the flesh of our bodies and the chemical processes that sustain our lives. Considering a person's emotional, spiritual, and physical well-being; you would value these aspects equally because they are inextricably intertwined. You would value the care of the body as much as the mental health of an individual. You would understand that spiritual connection does not necessitate worship of a deity and that the practice of living your life with care and concern for others as well as the self is the embodiment of spiritual elevation. When a person finds balance and health in their body, relationships, and connections to others, they are most well. This is what is described by the term holistic well-being.

Beginning a sex-affirming relationship with oneself

Now is a perfect time to question the status quo and defiantly embrace yourself as a sexual being. There is no better time to let go of the burden of shame within your life. Moments of shame could be replaced with joy and self-acceptance instead. You could feel lighter and happier simply by loving the skin you live in without judgment. If you find this to be difficult at first, keep using tools discussed in this text to examine your own beliefs and how they are affecting your being able to fully embrace yourself. Invite compassion to your words and thoughts. Consider the origins of your beliefs and choose self-love over hate. Choose to radically embrace loving yourself rather than allowing negative beliefs to diminish your essential being. Some people worry that if they were to become less self-critical, they may become too arrogant or that they would be deluding themselves to believe something other than what may have been repeated endless times in the past. By having an awareness of the emotional/mental programming that has been instilled within your mind, you are empowered to reevaluate and decide what you adopt as truth. You are not likely to become an egomaniac from simply entertaining the belief that you are acceptable as you are and that there is room for a variety of experiences in this world.

In a sex-positive world, sexuality would be celebrated as a joyous part of human existence. It would be honored as a source of connection between individuals and the world at large. How to adopt sex-positivity? Challenge assumptions regarding what expressions of sexuality are acceptable. Consider the source of these judgmental beliefs and examine the history behind them. This takes time and patience. However, being comfortable with who you are is worth the persistent effort of structuring new ways of thinking and navigating moments of discomfort. Consider how, if you were to continue living life as the person you have been told you should be as opposed to the person you really are, what would you have to sacrifice, hide, or deny to be acceptable? It begins with the desire to become your best self and continuing to amplify an inner voice of self-love and compassion.

When you notice beliefs that limit full appreciation for who you are, congratulate yourself for having noticed this thought and then consciously amend it toward kindness. Remember that it is not necessary to shower yourself with overly positive platitudes that you don't believe or can feel at this time but rather seek a kinder perspective that you can actually connect with as being true. The work of embracing yourself as a sexual being involves questioning what you have learned from family, society, religion, and other socializing influences. Typically, this is not an easy task. Many people who are just coming to the work of exploring their sexuality and adopting sex-positivity are doing so later in life and can sometimes feel embarrassed that it has taken them so long to come to this understanding. Again, invite compassion for a person who was given self-limiting beliefs before they had the full capacity to examine and decide for themselves what they understand to be true. If you have difficulty fostering a voice of self-compassion, imagine what you may say to someone you love and care for deeply. Would the statements you say to yourself be the same as those you may share with a best friend or beloved family member? Most likely, they would have more kindness. Using this alternate framing can be an effective tool in altering how you relate to yourself as a sexual human being if making the leap to self-affirmation is difficult at this time.

Now, what to do with all that information??

Understanding the myriad of social influences that affect a person's comfort with sexuality and self-acceptance is crucial to unlearning shame and its many tools of self-abasement. Shame degrades a person's ability to experience self-affirmation. From the moment you may have heard that you should dress in a certain way to avoid being judged negatively by others to the subtle suggestion that "good" girls don't do this or that, you have been socialized with judgments that harm or limit self-acceptance and expression. Some men may be able to relate to the unintended consequence of patriarchal shame surrounding societal measures of masculinity, dictating what is acceptable in terms of how you behave, present yourself, and specifically how you are expected to uphold the norms of "being a man." You are encouraged to express feelings of anger or stoicism but never tenderness, vulnerability, or willing submission. To do so is to forfeit your ability to be viewed as being a man. Fortunately, being aware of these biases allows you to reform previously held limiting beliefs and free yourself from unnecessary constraints that do not support your well-being. The idea of shedding these beliefs may be intimidating for some. That is ok. Take as much time as you need to process the hurtful beliefs that are negatively affecting you. You can both embrace the societal influences that make your life beautiful and fulfilling and shed shame regarding your experience of sexuality. Life is too short to live without the joy of loving yourself fully.

When you encounter beliefs that are stubborn to change, be patient and continue working to adopt a kinder and more loving self-concept. If you get stuck, think of someone you love dearly and consider what you may say to them if they were feeling similarly as yourself? Would you be as harsh? It is likely that you would try to be considerate of their feelings and not try to be blatantly hostile or cruel as the thoughts you allow your own mind to accept. Fortunately, as you continue to practice correcting beliefs/thoughts that diminish your humanity, it becomes easier to connect with the selflove you are seeking.

Once you have gained an awareness of these self-sabotaging thoughts, you can combat statements of what you "should" be doing or what you "must" be in order to be deemed acceptable. Recognize these nagging thoughts as instruments of guilt and shame. Use the tools of mindfulness and compassion to gently transform your thinking. Whenever you notice yourself thinking shame-based thoughts, give yourself praise for not letting this thought go unchecked! Without you noticing such thoughts, it would not be possible to adopt new ways of thinking. This is something to celebrate! Previously, such thoughts seemed wholly true and accurate; however, through consciously challenging thoughts related to sexual shame, you now have begun to embrace a more loving and accepting self-concept. When you are able, take the time to identify any evidence that confirms or denies the validity of your self-defeating thought and replace it with one that is more self-affirming. The thought record is an excellent tool to guide you through this process.

As you are wading through the years of negative programming you may have internalized regarding your gender, sexuality, or sexual orientation, utilize your awareness of these influences to shift your perspectives beyond self-limiting ones. If you are a person who embodies a marginalized identity, take this information to unlearn the messages that strip you of your authenticity and innate worth, even if it comes from your own cultural/social group. May it assist you with releasing layers of oppression that may have been internalized by living in a society that does not value all its members. If you are a person whose identity is valued by society, I hope this information is able to assist in unlearning messages you may have adopted from being socialized in a society that does not value the beauty of all cultures. Ridding oneself of judgmental and critical beliefs about others allows for greater self-acceptance as well. This cannot be overlooked. Our thoughts about others are often reflections of ourselves. We often are most critical of those who reflect aspects of ourselves that are unsettling. Through understanding the intersectionality of these societal influences, one can become free of biases that hinder a person's ability to enjoy being a sexual being without shame.

Nicole

AGE: 43, IDENTICAL TWIN, BLACK, YOGI, CISGENDERED, HETEROSEXUAL, MOTHER, BUSINESS OWNER

I grew up in a predominantly white upper-middle-class town and was raised by my parents, having an identical twin sister, an older sister, and an adopted brother. We attended Catholic school and were given further education by my parents in the arts and literature. My parents were very sweet and loving people who were all about service. Both were raised as Southern Baptists in Alabama. My dad was a deacon, and both he and my mom were very active in the church. We were involved in church activities most days of the week. My parents were committed to our upbringing and being of service to others in addition to their professional lives. My mother was an executive administrator to the CEO of General Motors, and my dad also worked for GM as a supervisor of the proving grounds. Needless to say, there were high standards and expectations in our household. They impressed upon us expectations of excellence and awareness of the importance of how you present yourself, not just representative of the self but of your family, community, and race, as well as the gravity of knowing that repercussions are greater being a Black child as compared to my white friends.

Although my parents were religious, they were not shaming of sex and created a sex-positive environment. The body was never something of shame. The female form is the most beautiful in nature. It is something to be looked at, and admired, to understand there is a beauty and elegance to it. When our bodies started to change, my parents made a point of showing us art depicting varied kinds of bodies, many shapes and forms. We were explained that "men in our family tend to look this way" and the proper names for the reproductive organs and what they do. There was never anything that we could not talk about. My mom even encouraged us to take a mirror and look at ourselves. She did not discourage us from exploring our bodies and understanding how we enjoy pleasure. She expressed the belief that you should touch yourself to know what those sensations are but that you should be the only one who should touch you and that we should immediately let her know if anyone attempted to do so in any inappropriate manner. My mom encouraged us to know what works for us and what doesn't, but also about the maturity and understanding that is needed to begin thinking about having sexual relationships. She talked about having the mental capacity to fully understand the magnitude of such choices.

When we were beginning to date around age 14-15, we were allowed out only with my twin, and the other person needed to bring a date or friend; you weren't going anywhere by yourself (Dad's rules). And as we were getting to know dates, they had to come by the house and talk a while with my parents. Once that was satisfied and questions were sufficiently answered, perhaps next time, the date could possibly be allowed to move to the couch in the living room. Mom and Dad were around but gave us space.

Now that my girls are entering adolescence, I am aware of not only the challenges of being a teenager but also how the challenges of my children are similar but also much different from my own. There are so many compelling influences in social media and society that are made to be far more important than what really matters. So, the house in which we are living is now named Oshun Manor (Oshun is a West African deity associated with love, sensuality, adornment, and femininity). In Oshun Manor, what we create here is our reality, not what someone else tells you or what you think you see out there in the world, online or on television. That's all fake. I don't watch TV. There is so much more you can be doing, living an actual life instead of watching someone create a fake situation online. It's important to me for them to be able to make that delineation.

With respect to the physical changes and experiences they are having, I talk to my girls very freely about what is going to happen to their bodies so they know what to expect. I've shared with them that when you have reached maturity to the point where you are inclined to have sexual relations, hopefully in a committed relationship, then they are able to make sound choices regarding how they wish to be sexual beings. This is something that has been an ongoing conversation that is open and based in love.

I want the best for my children, and something that I encourage other parents to adopt is to take a beat and check in with yourself, and attend to your own mental health needs. Although there are scenarios that are incredibly frustrating and tense, try to remember when you were their age, what their perspective could possibly be? Think in those moments about what you would like your relationship with your children to be when they are older and no longer in your home or in your direct care? Because, when you are in the thick of things, it's easy to respond in a certain way that could create a lingering negative effect on your long-term relationship. It's really easy to do. I try to operate with that thought, holding graceful elegance because I really do want to have my children in my life. We are given this huge responsibility of providing love, care, and protection for these dynamic beings who are closer to God than we are, I believe still. It's just worth it to take a pause and check in within yourself and understand that they are children. It is our duty to be kind and to operate in love and show them how to be loved in the world as opposed to being an outlet for anger and disappointment. Consider what to do or say to address problematic behavior, but you need to take a minute and do what you need to do to be your best for them. Go outside or send them away so you can recenter yourself to remember that they are babies who are in this crazy world and are depending on us to give them the best outcomes. It's not easy, and you may want to wring someone's neck, but that is not the best thing. It is our responsibility to grow in those moments.

CHAPTER ELEVEN
Ending legacies of sexual shame

How to not perpetuate stigma and shame surrounding sex and sexuality

For better or worse, most people were raised by well-meaning but imperfect parents who shared with you what they were taught or believed was the best way to live a good life. They may not have intended to instill the negative associations you may have regarding sexuality, yet nonetheless, somewhere along the way, you internalized the beliefs, teachings, and values of society and culture that shames sexuality. Many of our core beliefs about ourselves are formed before we have developed the verbal ability to create a narrative that makes sense of the world that surrounds us. However, these thoughts, regardless of validity, become the foundations upon which we formulate our understanding of the world. They develop into the structures of belief that color our perceptions of ourselves as compared to what we have been taught we should be.

Through working on eliminating these barriers to self-acceptance, you are now able to utilize your knowledge and awareness to fully embrace your most authentic self with unconditional love. Your commitment to freeing yourself from anything that is not self-affirming will begin to shine through you in ways that initially may not be obvious to others, but you can feel within yourself. There is something that is organically attractive about someone who radiates self-confidence and appreciation for others. It is not necessary that you proselytize the life-changing wonders of letting go of shame surrounding sex and sexuality. Your own journey of self-acceptance has positive benefits that extend beyond sexuality. This change permeates how you show up in your various roles, relationships, and, most importantly, for yourself. This allows a person to feel more at ease because they are no longer in conflict with themselves. Others may notice this positive shift within you as well. They may not understand why it is that you smile more and seem a bit brighter, but it shows.

Consequentially, it would be naïve to expect everyone in your life to understand why you have changed or that they may not reject you in some way. This hurts. However, this rejection also creates space where you may choose to prioritize relationships with people who are self-affirming. While this is typically not an instantaneous transition, with time, you will be able to cultivate connections with people who accept and appreciate who you are as a person. This transition can be isolating and challenging for some. Find sources of support, whether they be personal, virtual, or professional, knowing that nothing stays the same forever. You will emerge from this feeling more self-assured and whole.

Freedom from prioritizing the judgments of others is a self-affirmation. It validates your experience of being fully human and that your humanity is worthy of love. If there are people, ideologies, or influences that negate your inherent worth as a human being deserving of love, be critical and ask yourself if this relationship affirms or hinders your connection to self-love. The struggle to nurture love for yourself transforms your tolerance for things that do not bring your soul joy. Life is short. Each day, you are given the opportunity to choose to live in the fullness of your authentic self rather than some diminished version of yourself. This diminished façade wears you like a costume but does not feel the warmth of self-love and acceptance. It cannot. It may be a close facsimile of you, but does not shine with the same luminescence behind your eyes or freely laugh without self-conscious measurement. Not allowing yourself the joy of your humanity is a tragedy you have the power to influence. You can choose love over hate as a paradigm that guides your relationships with others, yourself included.

Despite our best efforts, we all make mistakes. Parents wanting to raise their children without the same burdens of shame may wish to create an environment that builds respect for themselves and others. Giving children unconditional love and the space for self-discovery nurtures healthy adults who are comfortable giving and receiving love. They are most likely to develop secure attachments to others when they receive reliable support and care. Additionally, securely attached adults who have the tools to navigate a sometimes hostile world with positive self-regard are more resilient. Although creating a utopia is impossible, we can positively influence the world around us. By being mindful of perpetuating shame regarding sexuality, you create a foundation for self-acceptance and potentially a world that celebrates the beauty of diverse human experiences.

Encouraging curiosity and exploration supports a person in understanding themselves without the biases of others. This ripple affects everyone around us, whether we realize it or not. The scourge of hate and discrimination in our current society can change as we support individuals in becoming their best selves. The powers that dictate how people are socialized are threatened by those who challenge norms because it threatens their power to control others in ways that benefit their inter-

You have a right to enjoy sexuality in ways that are best aligned with who you are as an individual. Only you can determine how you live your life. Living to please the standards or expectations of others leaves us feeling hollow and self-defeated. Our responsibility is to not harm others. Beyond that, embrace loving yourself and allowing sexuality to be a pleasurable experience you are free to enjoy.

Do no harm. This bears repeating for as long as humanity inflicts cruelty upon others. This practice begins with the awareness of thoughts that shape your opinions and views. Your thoughts naturally affect the words you use and how you communicate with others. This builds momentum when it joins forces with fear and exploitation that masquerades as virtue or politics. Hateful or judgmental thoughts should be met with the highest of skepticism if your opinions and views about others are based upon what you know solely from what others have told you, what media presents to you, or what you imagine some "other" person to be. Lived experience is something that cannot be replicated by anything other than that which is based in real-life connection. Meet people who do not initially appear to be like yourself. Approach people with curiosity about who they are, even if they seem superficially similar to you. If you notice yourself making assumptions, lean into learning more about whatever view this is based on. By being open to the possibility that what you know is not wholly true, you are able to utilize critical thinking to discover what you could know for yourself.

If you find that you have not been able to maneuver past problematic events or beliefs, you may benefit from seeking support from a therapist. It is important to find someone who has experience working with your concerns. Aside from the professional qualifications and education a person has attained, therapists are also people. This means that you will naturally connect with some people more than others. This is ok. What is most important is for you to feel comfortable being open and honest about your concerns. This openness facilitates the process of shedding self-defeating beliefs or patterns of behavior. Once you have found someone with whom you feel comfortable sharing intimate aspects of your life, be patient with yourself while you build the skills to navigate toward being able to enjoy the pleasures of sexuality and unconditional self-love.

Lastly, thank you for taking this journey to free yourself from sexual shame! I hope that the questions posed in this work allow you to explore the many dimensions that have shaped you as a person. You are not broken or defective. People who have experienced a multitude of harmful or traumatic events have also been able to reconstruct their beliefs to support loving themselves for who they are and joyful sexuality in their lives. You can too!

Bibliography

"Prevalence and Characteristics of Sexual Violence, Stalking, and Intimate Partner Violence Victimization — National Intimate Partner and Sexual Violence Survey, United States. CDC, 2011." Centers for Disease Control and Prevention. https://www.cdc.gov/mmwr/preview/mmwrhtml/ss6308a1.htm#:~:text=Prevalence%20of%20Sexual%20Violence%20Victimization,an%20estimated%2011.5%25%20of%20women.

Merriam-Webster, 2020. https://www.merriam-webster.com/dictionary/shame.

Brown, 2020. http://www.BreneBrown.com.

"Native American gender roles." Indian Health Service, 2020. https://www.ihs.gov/lgbt/health/twospirit/#:~:text=Traditionally%2C%20Native%20American%20two%20spirit,a%20distinct%2C%20alternative%20gender%20status

Mayer, L., & McHugh, P. "Sexuality and Gender findings from biological, psychological and social sciences." The New Atlantis. 2016. https://www.thenewatlantis.com/publications/part-three-gender-identity-sexuali-ty-and-gender.

BBC.com. "Do we need more than two genders?" 2020. https://www.bbc.com/news/health-35242180.

Noyola, N., Sánchez, M., & Cardemil, E. V. (2020). Minority stress and coping among sexual diverse Latinxs. Journal of Latinx Psychology, 8(1), 58–82. https://doi.org/10.1037/lat0000143

"Cultural look at colonialism, Christianity and sexual stigma." 2020. https://cultursmag.com/colonial-sexuality/.

Sue, D. (2010). Microaggressions and Marginality: Manifestations, Dynamics, and Impact. John Wiley & Sons.

Dictionary.com, 1/16/21. https://www.dictionary.com/browse/respectability-politics

Reuters, 2020, 2/12/21.

https://www.reuters.com/article/us-colorado-priests-sexabuse/catholic-church-pays-7-million-to-victims-in-colorado-of-sexual-abuse-by-priests-idUSKBN28C04C

Sinead O'Connor Image. https://www.dailyedge.ie/sinead-oconnor-pope-3632821-Oct2017/

Rape culture in the workplace: https://archive.thinkprogress.org/rape-culture-at-work-five-examples-of-how-employers-turn-women-into-sex-objects-ea0a0f636242/

McMahon, Sarah. (2007). Understanding Community Specific Rape Myths: Exploring Student Athlete Culture. https://womens-studies.rutgers.edu/images/stories/Faculty_Image/Understandingcommunityspecificrapemyths.pdf

Boscamp, Emi. 2020. What is rape culture? 10 Examples of what it looks like. https://www.mindbodygreen.com/0-21715/12-ways-we-all-contribute-to-rape-culture-without-realizing-it.html

Genderbread Person. 2021. https://www.itspronouncedmetrosexual.com/2018/10/the-genderbread-per-son-v4/

Time, 2012. https://time.com/3001785/todd-akin-legitimate-rape-msnbc-child-of-rape/

UCLA, 2022. https://williamsinstitute.law.ucla.edu/press/ncvs-trans-press-release/

Polaris, 2022. https://polarisproject.org/wp-content/uploads/2019/09/LGBTQ-Sex-Trafficking.pdf

Healthline, 2022. https://www.healthline.com/health/what-are-chakras#the-7-main-chakras

NIH.gov, 2018. https://www.ncbi.nlm.nih.gov/pmc/articles/PMC5797481/

Sciencedaily.com, 2019. https://www.sciencedaily.com/releases/2019/06/190610151934.htm

More Reference sites http://www.articleworld.org/index.php/Chastity_belt
http://www.articleworld.org/index.php/True_Love_Waits

Green Hill, 2022. https://greenhillrecovery.com/toxic-masculinity-vs-healthy-masculinity/ NIH.gov, 2017. https://www.ncbi.nlm.nih.gov/pmc/articles/PMC5709795/

Globalgrind.com, 2023. https://globalgrind.com/182718/a-list-of-republicans-that-got-caught-in-gay-scandals/

Logotv.com, 2023. https://www.logotv.com/news/lpa6sk/19-republican-politicians-gay-sex

PNAS.org, 2023. https://www.pnas.org/doi/10.1073/pnas.2000333117

NCSL.org, 2023. https://www.ncsl.org/health/state-policies-on-sex-education-in-schools#:~:text=Twenty%2Dtwo%20states%20require%20that,medically%2C%20factually%20or%20technically%20accurate

American Journal of Psychiatry, 2022. https://ajp.psychiatryonline.org/doi/10.1176/appi.ajp-rj.2022.180103#:~:text=In%20the%20first%20edition%20of,personality%20disturbance%E2%80%9D%20(1)

Psychiatrist.com, 2023. https://www.psychiatrist.com/jcp/depression/sexual-dysfunction/circuits-sexual-desire-hypoactive-sexual-desire-disorder/#:~:text=Sexual%20excitation%20is%20hypothetically%20mediated,norepinephrine%2C%20oxytocin%2C%20and%20melanocortins

Grunge.com, 2023. https://www.grunge.com/621469/heres-why-hitler-was-rejected-from-art-school/

PornHub.com, 2023. https://www.pornhub.com/video/search?search=sex+education

The Thought Record, 2023. www.getselfhelp.co.uk

Anti-Gay Laws, 2023. https://antigaylaws.org/regional/africa/ BBC.com, 2023. https://www.bbc.com/news/world-43822234

Statista.com, 2023. https://www.statista.com/statistics/1269999/criminalization-of-same-sex-relations-in-africa/

Gendered Innovations.stanford.edu, 2023. https://genderedinnovations.stanford.edu/terms/intersectionality.html

Bailey, M., & Mobley, I. A. (2019). Work in the Intersections: A Black Feminist Disability Framework. Gender & Society, 33(1), 19-40. https://doi.org/10.1177/0891243218801523

Ziegler, A., Matsick, J. L., Moors, A. C., Rubin, J., & Conley, T. D. (2014). Does monogamy harm women? Deconstructing monogamy with a feminist lens. [Special Issue on Polyamory].Journal für Psychologie, 22(1),

-18

Additional citations

Frigerio, A., Ballerini, L. & Valdés Hernández, M. Structural, Functional, and Metabolic Brain Differences as a Function of Gender Identity or Sexual Orientation: A Systematic Review of the Human Neuroimaging Literature. Arch Sex Behav 50, 3329–3352 (2021). https://doi.org/10.1007/s10508-021-02005-9Brain differences between cis and transgendered people: https://link.springer.com/article/10.1007/s10508-021-02005-9

www.ingramcontent.com/pod-product-compliance
Lightning Source LLC
Chambersburg PA
CBHW080523030426
42337CB00023B/4613